Big Horses,
Good Dogs,
and
Straight Fences

Big Horses, Good Dogs, and Straight Fences

Musings of Everyday Ranch Life

Mark Rashid

Johnson Books
BOULDER

Spring Creek Press
ESTES PARK

Published by Johnson Books, a division of Big Earth Publishing, 3005 Center Green Drive, Suite 220, Boulder, Colorado 80301.
E-mail: books@bigearthpublishing.com
www.bigearthpublishing.com
1-800-258-5830

Cover design: Constance Bollen, cbgraphics
Cover photos: Wendy Rashid
Text design and composition: Eric Christensen

9 8 7 6 5 4 3 2

Library of Congress Cataloging-in-Publication Data
   Big horses, good dogs, and straight fences: musings of everyday ranch life / Mark Rashid.
      p. cm.
   ISBN 1-55566-390-7
   1. Ranch Life—Colorado—Anecdotes. 2. Ranching—Colorado—Anecdotes. 3. Rashid, Mark. I. Title.
   SF197.4.R37 2006
   636'.01092–dc22   2006017857

Printed in the United States of America

In memory of Sadie and Patch ...
two very good dogs.

Contents

Preface

I believe just about everybody has a time in their life they can look back on with fondness and appreciation, even though that time may not have been filled with overwhelming achievement or incredible success. What you are about to read in this book, *Big Horses, Smart Dogs, and Straight Fences,* is a sampling of one of those periods in my life … a time I most certainly look back on with fondness and appreciation.

This was a fun book for me to write because as I jotted down the various stories with input on which ones to include from my wife, Wendy, it allowed the two of us to revisit a time and place that really no longer exists except in our memories. It was in the years right after Wendy and I got married … when our kids were small, our dogs were young, and I was spending a lot of time working at or helping out on various cattle ranches and horse operations in and around Estes Park, Colorado, where we live.

Whenever Wendy and I get together with friends from back in those days, it seems there are certain stories that always get told and retold. The stories usually come up after supper, when the meal has been eaten, the dishes have been done, and everything has been cleaned up and put away. It's then everybody seems to migrate to the kitchen, and in amongst all the recent news about work and family, someone will inevitably say something like: "Hey, remember when …" And the next thing you know, we're off and running.

As you will soon see, the subject matter of these stories varies widely and covers topics such as building fences, kids, ponies, kids *and* ponies, draft horses, working cattle, and guiding in the mountains … just to name a few. Of course, even though the subject matter helps make a good story, it is often the individuals who were there when the story actually became a story that make it worth telling.

In this book, you will get a chance to meet some of those folks who helped make these events worth remembering and telling. You'll meet my good friend Dwight, a rancher who is one of the best teamsters I've ever met and who continues to hold my utmost respect, even after all these years. You'll meet Chef John, who learned the hard way about a dog's loyalty, and you'll meet my friend Wil (not his real name, for reasons that will become apparent).

You'll also meet the animals that helped bring life to the stories as well … the dun colt; my draft horses Diamond and Andy; Sam, the pony; our dogs, Sadie, Patch, and Bill; and a few good saddle horses to boot. Heck, with a cast of characters like that, how can you possibly go wrong?

Still, no matter how good the story or how interesting the subject matter, in the end, a story is only a story when there's someone there to hear it. It is for that reason I truly thank you for picking up this book and giving it a read. I hope you will enjoy it as much as I've enjoyed bringing it to you.

CHAPTER 1

The Slippery Trailer

"When in doubt, trust your horse."

As I stood there at the back of the trailer with rain pouring off the brim of my hat in a steady stream of brownish water, I tried unsuccessfully to convince myself that I wasn't really all that tired. I may have been better off trying to convince myself I wasn't all that wet.

It was rodeo week, and that meant my already heavy workload had doubled. At the time I was the livery supervisor at a local guest ranch, and that job alone usually kept me pretty well occupied for the better part of the day. In addition to my regular job, during this week we had been contracted to be at every rodeo performance—one in the afternoon and one in the evening for four days straight—with our four-up of Belgian draft horses.

Our task at the rodeo was to load the barrels for the barrel race onto our big wagon. We would trot our hitch of drafts out into the arena, drop the barrels off nonstop, so they could be set up in the barrel pattern, and then trot back out. Once the barrel race was over, we would trot the hitch back into the arena, pick the barrels up again, and haul them back out.

Admittedly, when you say it like that, it doesn't sound like all that much work. And if the truth were known, that part of the deal wasn't that much work. The work was in everything that led up to taking the hitch out into the arena: washing and grooming four horses the size of half-ton pickup trucks, making sure all the harness was clean and adjusted properly, inspecting and washing the wagon before every performance, and getting

1

the teams harnessed and hitched to the wagon. We also had to make sure the barrels (which were painted to look like over-sized Coors beer cans) were in place and ready for us to pick up.

After we made our run in and out of the arena, it was time to get the barrels back to their proper storage place, park the wagon and unhitch the teams, groom the horses, get the harnesses put up properly, inspect the wagon again, put the horses up, and make sure they had feed and water. Once all that was done, it was time to start getting ready for the next performance, which on most days was only four hours later.

During our four-hour break, I would hightail it the seven miles back to the ranch to make sure everything was still heading in the same direction I had pointed it in the morning before I left, smooth out any bumps that may have come up, and then turn around and head right back to the rodeo grounds in time to wash the teams, clean the harness, and … well, you get the idea.

I have to admit, it was a nice show for the audience, which was usually full of summertime tourists who might have never seen a hitch of draft horses, and it was also good exposure for the ranch. Plus, I really liked it anytime I could work with my big horses.

♘   ♘

This was our third year "doing the barrels," as we had come to call it, and I have to admit, the shine was starting to wear off a little. The first year was a lot of fun, mostly because it gave us another opportunity to use our four-up besides the occasional parade or the odd times in winter when the snow got too deep for one team to pull our big sleigh.

The second year, while still fun, was a little more difficult be-cause a number of things had come up at the ranch that needed tending at the same time I was supposed to be doing the barrels. It had been touch and go a couple of times during the week, but luckily we were still able to get everything done.

But this third year ... this one was different. The week had started with the annual rodeo parade on Wednesday morning. The weather was pleasant, and I didn't sweat too much, so that was good. The first performance later that afternoon went off without any trouble, and so did the one later that evening. But the next run ... that's when everything kind of began to go a little sideways.

There were very few clouds in the sky that Thursday morning. Even so, there was just a hint of too much humidity in the air, which almost always meant rain was on the way. Sure enough, during the afternoon performance, just after the calf roping, the sky began to look sinister with those heavy, dark clouds that told you, *Before the day is over, someone is going to get wet.*

The rain had been kind enough to hold off for most of the rodeo, but as luck would have it, just as we entered the gate to take the barrels into the arena, the sky opened up like it was mad at the ground. And there we were, with our slickers back at the barn. We hadn't gone five feet before we were all soaked to the bone.

Normally, this wouldn't have been much of an issue. After all, it wasn't the first time we'd worked in the rain. But for some reason that day was different. Andy, the left-hand horse on the wheel team, seemed to take offense at the sudden downpour and, as a result, began to shake his head uncontrollably while bucking in place. In fact, he'd been a little fidgety almost as soon as we put his harness on that day, but it was nothing like what he started doing once it began to rain.

I urged the hitch forward, and the horses, with the exception of Andy, responded without hesitation. Andy tried hard to stand in place and buck, but the combined power of the other three simply pulled him along. The other horses swung into a high-stepping rhythmic trot, while Andy broke into slow, choppy canter. Leaning into the stinging, cold rain coming directly into our faces, we dropped the first barrel in position and made a wide swing to the left toward the second drop.

Andy was a good-sized horse, about 17.2 hands tall and just a hair over 2,200 pounds. His partner Diamond, however, was bigger. At 18.1 hands and right around 2,600 pounds, he was one of the biggest Belgian draft horses in the state at the time, and he didn't seem to take too kindly to Andy's shenanigans. As I swung the hitch into position to drop the second barrel, Diamond reached across and hit Andy in the side of the neck with the top of his head. This caused Andy to jump to his left, buck, and nearly get his left hind foot over the tug that connected him to the doubletree.

When Andy jumped, he pulled the tongue of the wagon to the left just enough to send the back of the wagon into the smallest of fishtails. We must have been quite a sight to the crowd (some 1,500 strong), because they spontaneously burst into the loudest barrage of applause I had ever heard. I suppose the sight of four big horses kicking up dust and mud, with the two back ones knocking each other around, the wagon fishtailing, and the driver and his assistant soaked to the bone with their hats tipped into the wind and rain, must have been more than they could stand.

Somehow we got the second barrel dropped off pretty much where it was supposed to go and made our final swing to drop off the last barrel, the one closest to the grandstand. As we charged past and got near our drop-off point, the applause from the crowd grew even louder. This seemed to unnerve the usually unflappable lead team, Woodrow and Gus. As we neared the drop-off point, Woody, who was on the right-hand side and closest to the crowd, shied into Gus, causing both of them to pull to the left, which took my wheel team to the left as well.

The bad news was we dropped the barrel, but missed our drop-off point by a good twelve feet. The good news was we had swung so far to the left that by the time I got both teams back in line, we were heading straight for the exit gate, which we made without any trouble at all, as the crowd whistled and cheered at what I'm sure they thought was a spectacularly pre-planned, almost-out-of-control run.

♘ ♘

After exiting the arena I brought the horses back down to a walk, turned them around for our pick-up run, and pulled them to a stop. I handed the lines to my assistant, Susie Heidi, whose job it was to keep the excess of the four driving lines, which hung off the seat behind me, straight and untangled, something she'd done to perfection during the run. Then I climbed down to check for any damage to the horses and equipment.

A quick look around showed that everything was okay, and other than a superficial nick on Andy's right hind fetlock, all the horses seemed to be just fine physically. As soon as we had pulled to a stop, all the horses, with the exception of Andy, had characteristically dropped their heads and relaxed. Andy, how-ever, was still shaking his head, switching his tail, snorting, and prancing in place.

It was strange because I'd never seen him act like that before, even though we had worked together in weather that was often-times much worse than what we had that day. I went to his head and took hold of the line attached to his bit and just sort of stood there with him, mostly to make sure he didn't just decide to run off, but also in hopes that my presence at his head might help quiet him. Before long, he stopped his prancing but continued to snort, stomp his left hind foot, and swish his tail.

I'm not sure how many barrel racers there were that day, but after several had made their runs, they were finally down to the last two or three contestants, and Andy wasn't much better. As a sort of afterthought, not really wanting a repeat of our last run if it could be helped, I decided to take a quick look at his har-ness, just to make sure there wasn't a problem with it. I started at his bridle and went back to his collar and hames, through his harness to his britching, and finally to his crupper.

And it was there, under his crupper, that I found the culprit. Somehow a small sliver of needle-sharp straw had gotten caught up under his crupper and embedded itself in the soft skin just under his tail. Any time he swished his tail or the crupper moved, it must have moved the little sliver, which I'm sure irritated him to no end.

"Dang," I said, as I slowly lifted his tail with my left hand to get a better look.

"That's the last one," Susie announced, as the last barrel racer entered the arena.

"Just a minute," I said, as the rain fell harder.

I reached up and cautiously took the inch-long sliver between the thumb and index finger of my right hand. Andy stomped his foot and offered to kick at me. I gently moved my fingers up as close to the skin as possible. Then, without moving my hand, I squeezed the sliver between my fingers, moved my finger tips toward the palm of my hand, and smoothly removed the splinter.

Andy violently shook his head and stomped his foot. I took a quick look at the sliver, which was tinged crimson for about an eighth of an inch where it had been imbedded. Then I quickly swung back up onto the seat of the wagon, took the lines, and adjusted them in my hands for our next run. As I did, Andy's head slowly dropped, his feet squared up, and he settled into his harness and quietly waited for direction.

Our final run, even though the wind had picked up and the arena was a slippery, muddy mess, was smooth and uneventful. It probably wasn't as much fun for the crowd to watch, but it sure was a whole lot easier on my nerves, as well as on the horses and equipment.

U U

While the rain and bad weather (certainly uncharacteristic for mid-July in our little town) let up some over the next couple days, it never did get dry or warm enough to encourage a lot of tourists to come and watch a rodeo. As a result, spectator attendance dropped off considerably over the next three performances.

By Saturday morning our wagon, horses, and harness, as well as ourselves, were pretty well waterlogged. The final rodeo performance was going to be held later that afternoon, and with the rain clouds already settling in along the valley and hovering low over the rodeo grounds, it looked like we were going to be in for another soaker.

About ten-thirty that morning I decided rather than getting two teams, complete with harness, soaked yet again, I'd just take one of the teams home and use the other for the final afternoon performance. We had been up late the night before cleaning and oiling both sets of harness after getting them rain-soaked, and we figured if we only used one team, that meant having to clean and oil only one set of harness.

To take that thought a step further, if we used the smaller team, Woodrow and Gus, we'd have less harness to clean, as their harness was much smaller than Diamond and Andy's.

So that's how I came to be standing at the back of the trailer with brownish rainwater pouring off the brim of my hat. I had noticed that when it rained real hard, as it had over the last three days, the water that came off my hat was always discolored, partly because it was washing away the dirt and grime that had been collecting during the dry season and partly because it was probably washing away some of the dye from the beaver felt.

As that brownish water streamed past my nose, I let out a long, drawn-out yawn, while I waited for my good friend, Dwight, to bring Andy out of the barn so we could load him and take him back to the ranch. Dwight is an excellent horseman and teamster in his own right, and for years we had been helping each other out whenever one or the other of us needed a hand. Not surprisingly, Dwight happened to show up that day, just when I could really use a little help.

I had already loaded Diamond, and he was standing tied in the nose of the twenty-four-foot stock trailer when Dwight offered to go and get Andy. As tired as I was, standing still for just a few minutes, even in the pouring rain, sounded better to me than walking the fifty or so yards back to the barn, so I happily agreed to let Dwight bring him out.

A couple minutes later, Dwight and Andy came out of the barn and sloshed their way over to the trailer.

"I'll take him," I said to Dwight, as they reached me.

Dwight handed me Andy's lead rope, and we switched positions so he could hold the door open against the west wind that kept trying to close it.

The ranch had recently bought the trailer but had not yet been able to purchase rubber floor mats for it. The bare wooden floor was wet and slick from the last three days of constant rain. Coupled with the fact that our big horses had caulks on the toes and heels of their shoes (the caulks gave the horses more traction on soft surfaces like dirt or gravel but also lessened considerably the area the foot made contact with on flat, hard surfaces), the lack of rubber mats turned out to be a recipe for disaster.

I led Andy into the trailer and was about halfway in with him when I suddenly heard, over the din of rain on the trailer roof, the unmistakable sound of Andy slipping on the floor behind me. The last thing I remember was turning around, watching all four of his feet going in different directions, and then seeing him, in an effort to regain his balance, lunge forward.

The next thing I remember was sitting in the passenger seat of the truck, with Dwight driving us back to the ranch and the wipers feebly flicking the unrelenting rain off the windshield. My hat, crumpled and bent, was sitting in my lap.

"What happened?" I asked. The movement of my jaw caused a dull pain to engulf nearly the entire left side of my face.

"I already told you," he said.

"Oh," I winced at the pain in my temple and looked out the truck window at the soaked landscape.

"You okay?" Dwight asked, after driving another mile or so.

"Yeah, I think so." My hand instinctively moved to the pain on the left side of my face.

"You know where you are?" he asked, throwing a glance in my direction.

"Looks like," I paused to make sure, "we're heading to the ranch."

"Well, good thing it was only your head," Dwight chuckled. "Anywhere else and you might have really got hurt."

I laughed without really knowing why.

"What happened?" I asked again.

I would later find out that Dwight had actually told me what happened at least five times since the incident had occurred, but this was the first time I would remember.

"That Andy horse got to slippin' on that wood floor and fell over right on top of you," he said. "Slammed you into the side of the trailer. Looked like he killed you, 'cuz you dropped like a rock and landed right underneath him when he was scramblin' around in there. How he didn't step on you when you were down, I'll never know. It was touch and go there for a little while. He let me ease in after he finally stopped movin' around, so I grabbed your feet and dragged you out from under him."

"I was underneath him?" I asked, a little surprised.

"You sure were," he said. "He never flinched when I went to pull you out, neither."

We started up the side of the mountain that would eventually lead us back to the ranch. Things were pretty quiet in the truck for another couple miles.

"That Andy horse … " Dwight finally said, as he eased the floor shift to a lower gear, "that's one damn good horse."

"Yes," I nodded, as I watched a bead of water making its way down the passenger-side window. "He is."

U U

I've thought about that day a lot over the years and just can't help wondering if Andy did what he could to help me out that day because I had helped him out when he needed it just a couple days before. I guess I'll never really know for sure.

One thing I do know for sure, however, was after that one particular rodeo week all those years ago, the relationship between Andy and me was never the same again. Even to this day, I can't help but smile every time I think about that big horse … and the effort he must have made to keep me safe as I lay helpless on that rain-soaked trailer floor.

CHAPTER 2

Two Good Dogs

"All it is, is patience."

We have good dogs. Now I know pretty much everybody who owns dogs thinks their dogs are good, too. And I suppose their dogs probably are real nice. But I've got to tell you, we've got *real* good dogs.

Several years ago I took our dogs to the pasture. It was mid-February and time to gather the horses so we could do mid-winter foot trimming and deworming. At the time we had three dogs: Sadie, who was a black lab/springer spaniel mix; Patch, a border collie; and Bill, a border collie/Australian shepherd cross.

On this particular trip, Sadie stayed home. Not because I didn't like her or didn't want her to come along, because I did. It's just that the other two dogs knew how to behave around livestock. And Sadie … well, Sadie, with a serious lack of herding instinct and in a sincere effort to do everything she could to help out during a gather, inadvertently spent most of her time and energy scattering whatever livestock you were trying to bring in. Then, of course, the herding dogs would go back out and re-gather the herd, and Sadie would scatter them again.

As you can imagine, that usually ended up being a long day. Because I really didn't want to do this job more than once on that particular day, I opted to leave Sadie home.

At the time, we had just over seventy head of horses on three different pastures that totaled a little over 700 acres. The pasture we were heading for was the smallest of the three, being about eighty acres. It was sort of rectangular in shape, with the long

11

sides being on the north and south. The gate was on the east end of the pasture and a dirt road ran along the south side clear to the west end, where there was an eighty-foot catch pen built out of lodgepole pine.

It had just been dumb luck in the past that most times I went to gather the herd, the horses would be grazing somewhere around the middle of the pasture. I usually drove to the west end and parked my pickup near the catch pen. Then I'd walk out and catch one of the horses, usually my gelding Buck, take him back to the pickup, saddle him up, and use him to gather the rest. Because the herd was already halfway to the pen, that part was always pretty easy.

When the dogs were with me, they would help by keeping the herd bunched up and moving slowly toward the catch pen. It was clear they thought this was a very important job, and they took it very seriously.

At the time of this particular gather, the horses on the pasture had wintered there for five or six years in a row, and so they pretty much knew the drill. They would bunch up when asked and then move west toward the catch pen. There was a small, four-foot, walk-through gate along the westernmost fence line that the horses had to go through to enter the catch pen.

Everything normally went pretty smooth with the only potential for trouble being when they were waiting their turn to go through the gate. That was when the possibility of them spilling was the greatest, particularly if there were any new horses in the herd.

Early spring along the Front Range of Colorado is always a crapshoot as far as the weather goes. It could be sixty degrees and sunny, or it could be twenty below and blowing snow. This particular day was right in the middle, about forty degrees, sunny, but no wind—just about the perfect day for trimming horses.

As I pulled through the gate that morning, the only problem I could see was that the whole herd was grazing down at the northeast corner of the pasture. Now normally I would have just gotten out of the truck, haltered up a horse, gotten back in the truck, and holding the lead rope out the truck window, taken the horse with me as I drove to the west end of the pasture. Unfortunately, the road was narrow, rutted, and flanked by huge cottonwood trees only inches from the road. Leading a horse next to or even behind my truck would have been not only foolhardy, but dangerous.

This meant I'd have to drive all the way down to the west end of the pasture and park the truck, which had all the dewormer in it and needed to be where the horses would eventually end up, walk all the way back to the east end, catch one horse, walk or ride it back to the west end, saddle the horse, ride back to the east end, and start the gather. By the time I reached the west end of the pasture and parked the truck, I had already decided that was going to be too much work.

It was probably the fourth or fifth time the dogs had been along to help with the gather on this pasture, and as I dropped the tailgate of the pickup to let them out, it was clear by the look on their faces they knew exactly why they were there. I decided, what the heck, why not let them try to gather the herd by themselves. They were great working dogs, although both were relatively young at the time and hadn't really worked a herd without direction from me.

Both dogs sat eagerly at the edge of the pickup bed, their ears erect and eyes intensely focused on me.

"Okay," I said.

In the blink of an eye, they were both on the ground running small, tight circles around my legs. As I started walking in the direction of the herd, they immediately fell in behind me, Bill on my right, Patch on my left.

We could not see the horses on the northeast end of the pasture from where we were, because the elevation in the center of the pasture was ten feet higher than at either end. The rise was so gradual it was deceiving, but it completely blocked our view of the herd.

I gazed off in the general direction of the herd and nodded my head.

"Bring 'em to me," I said.

The phrase "away to me" is actually the traditional command for a working dog to begin a gather. However, one of the first times Patch and I were working stock years before—just a couple head of cattle in a small pen—I used the term "bring them to me" after she had instinctively gathered the steers and was already moving them right where they needed to go—toward a gate I was standing beside. The command just sort of stuck, and I ended up using it any time I needed one of the dogs to bring an animal or group of animals in my general direction.

Upon hearing the command, both dogs took off running for all they were worth in the direction of my gaze. They only went about twenty yards, though, before stopping and turning back to look at me, almost as if to say, *Are you sure? We don't see anything out there!*

I kept my gaze on the northeastern horizon and repeated the command, "Bring 'em to me."

In unison, both dogs turned and took off in a wide circle toward the southeast. Now, having the dogs head in a different direction from where the herd was might be a little unnerving to someone who hasn't been around working dogs. In fact, that is exactly what we want them to do, and I was happy to see them do it on their own.

You see, if dogs run directly at a herd (as I'm sure Sadie would have done had she been there), they are going to spill the herd for sure. However, if the dogs take a wide berth, going around the herd and then coming up behind them, they can easily work the herd back in the proper direction. Even if the herd does spill, which isn't likely when the dogs are working well, they will at least spill in the direction we want them to be going.

Within a few seconds, both dogs, still running for all they were worth, disappeared over the little rise in the center of the pasture.

Okay, I thought to myself. *It should take them about five minutes to get to the other end of the pasture and get the herd bunched up. Probably another five to get them moving, and another five after that before I see them coming over the rise. So if I don't see anything in about fifteen minutes, I better go looking.*

I looked at my watch. *Yup, fifteen minutes ought to be just about right. After all, there's only twenty-two head over there. They shouldn't have too much trouble with just that many.*

I went back to the truck, got the deworming medicine out of the cab, and placed it on the tailgate. While I was doing that, it dawned on me that I should probably be in a position where the dogs could see me, should they come back looking for direction.

I looked at my watch. They'd been gone two minutes.

I walked out about two hundred yards to the northeast and watched for signs of life. I looked down at my watch once again. Four minutes had gone by. I strolled about thirty feet to the north, keeping my eyes on the horizon, and then turned and walked back to the south. Five minutes had passed. Now I considered myself a fairly patient person, so it was a little surprising when I started getting this thought in my head that maybe I should be seeing some progress from the dogs by now ... even though I had just told myself it would probably take fifteen minutes before I was likely to see them again.

♘ ♘

Hmm. I thought to myself. *Five minutes.* I looked back to the horizon—still no signs of life.

Well, five minutes isn't really all that much time, and besides, the herd was a little spread out. I turned and walked back to the north. *I'm sure they're fine.*

A few more minutes passed, and I could feel a hint of worry creep into my consciousness. It was the first time the two dogs were working a herd on their own, and they were pretty young dogs, after all. I walked back toward the south. Seven minutes had passed.

Seven minutes. Heck, anything could happen in seven minutes! Aw, man, what if they found a rabbit? They could be a mile away by now trying to chase a dang rabbit down a hole somewhere. Or a duck ... there's lots of ducks in the ditch along the road. Sadie got in trouble one time chasing a duck into the ditch. Broke through some thin ice, and I had to rope her to get her out. Dang, I hope they didn't go chasing ducks ... OR rabbits!

By then I had turned and was walking back to the north. *Eight-and-a-half minutes. I stopped and fixed my eyes on the horizon once again. Still no sign of the dogs or the horses.*

I bet they found a rabbit. Maybe they just wandered off. They could have done that, too.

I finally resigned myself to the fact that sending two young dogs off by themselves was probably not the smartest thing I'd ever done, and it was probably time for me to go look for them. With a hint of urgency in my step, I trudged off in the direction the dogs had gone nearly ten minutes before, kicking myself for thinking they would be able to handle the job I'd sent them to do.

It had not escaped me that I still had a pretty full day's work in front of me once the herd was gathered, which I was thinking I should have just gone ahead and done myself. Then, on top of all that work, I was going to have to go hunt up my lost dogs—something I wouldn't have had to do had I just not been so lazy in the first place.

I was still sort of muttering to myself and closing in on the middle of the pasture when I looked up and (much to my surprise) saw one horse, then another, heading my direction. I slowed to a stop and kept watching. Another horse showed up, then another, then three more, and six more behind them. Behind them was the rest of the herd, with Patch and Bill easing the horses along.

Patch is a very distinctive-looking border collie, being almost completely white with the only black on her being the characteristic border-collie mask, one small patch of black on her left side, and another at the head of her tail. Bill, on the other hand, is all black, with the traditional white cape over his shoulders and white on his legs.

It was easy to distinguish the two of them as they worked the herd. Patch would start on the right flank of the herd and ease her way behind them until she had made her way to the left flank. Bill would start on the left flank of the herd and ease his way behind them until he had made his way over to the right flank.

Once in a while one of the dogs would dodge or duck toward one of the horses that was thinking about getting out of line or perhaps offering to make a break for it, thus keeping the herd moving smoothly toward the west end of the pasture.

I took a quick glance at my watch. Thirteen minutes had passed since I first sent the dogs off on their maiden mission, two minutes shy of the time I had originally estimated.

I quietly and somewhat humbly watched as the dogs eased the herd past me. They both acknowledged me with quick glances, but they were way too busy for idle chat and kept the herd moving toward their destination.

I took a little shortcut back to the pen and got there just as the dogs bunched the herd up along the western fence line. The gate was already open, and I moved to a position about 60 feet north of the pen and about 100 feet from the western fence, keeping the herd between the fence and myself.

I pointed to the gate.

"Put 'em in," I said.

With Bill holding the herd, Patch eased in and quietly cut two horses out and escorted them through the gate. She stopped and looked at me. I looked at the herd, and she immediately went back to them, cut out three more, and escorted them through the gate.

By this time, all that was left in the herd were the old timers—the horses who had wintered on this pasture for years and knew the drill. One by one they fell into a single-file line and headed for the gate. With that, I called both dogs, and they immediately broke off the herd and took up positions behind me. Once the horses were all in the pen, I went over, with the dogs following close behind, and closed the gate.

That was the first opportunity I had to let the dogs know how much I appreciated the good job they had done and perhaps to let them know how foolish I felt to have doubted them.

The rest of the work that day went real easy, for both the dogs and me. For my part, the deworming and trimming went like clockwork, and we had all that finished up by mid-afternoon. For their part, the dogs spent the rest of the day laying in the shade of the pickup, drinking cold water from the ditch, and occasionally snapping at a horse or two that happened to put their nose a little too close to the grass outside the catch pen fence.

Yessir, it was a very good day.

♘ ♘

Nowadays, as much as I hate to say it, both dogs are a little older and a little arthritic and have slowed down considerably. Yet there are times when we're all just hanging out together when I think back to that day and how I learned something about the dedication of a good working dog … and the patience of a human.

CHAPTER 3

The Pony Ride

"A good horse is never a bad color."

During one of the winter meetings with the owner of the guest ranch where I was foreman, he asked if there was anything we needed for the horse program before the upcoming summer season got started. I told him there was—a pony.

At the time, the ranch catered mostly to families, and while we had horses for pretty much any skill level, age, and size of rider, the one thing we lacked was a pony for the really little kids, the kids who were too small or too young to go on trail rides but too big not to want to ride a real horse.

"A pony?" the owner questioned. "Why do we need a pony when we've got Chief?"

Chief was a thirty-six-year-old paint horse that the ranch had owned since before the current owner bought the ranch. He was a kind and gentle horse that still had a few teeth, as well as knots on his knees and a lot of gray hair around his eyes and muzzle. He was no longer able to go out on the trails, because he just couldn't physically do it anymore. However, he was still fit for very light work, so he had been charged with the task of performing pony rides.

Chief really seemed to enjoy his job, and he always took extra care when one of those little kids was up on his back. Being safe wasn't the issue at all. The problem was Chief was a relatively tall horse—a little over fifteen hands—and for some of the smaller kids, well, his size was just too intimidating. As a result, many little kids would leave the ranch having never had a chance to even sit on a horse, much less ride one (even if a "ride" was just being led around the arena).

For that reason, I felt we needed to get a real live pony, a pony small enough that nearly any little kid wouldn't be afraid to sit on it; good natured enough that it wouldn't mind the yelling, screaming, poking, and prodding that little kids almost always do once they are around ponies; and well mannered enough that it wouldn't bite, kick, rear, run off, or do anything else that might be considered not-so-good pony behavior when someone was handling or riding it.

"How much would a pony like that go for?" my boss asked.

"Hard to say," I shrugged. "If we're lucky, I suppose somewhere between a hundred and two hundred dollars."

He looked off into space for a few seconds, giving the idea some careful thought, and then slowly nodded.

"If you can find one for under two, go ahead," he said. "No renegades, though … understand?"

"I won't buy anything that isn't exactly what we're looking for," I reassured him.

A few weeks later I ran into my vet and let him know we were looking for a pony. I asked him to keep an eye out while on his rounds and give us a call if he saw anything that might work for us. I did the same thing with my farrier, Rick, when he was out to trim the horses.

Rick told me he knew of one pony for sale, and he thought the little guy might be perfect for what we needed. He dug around in the cab of his pickup and found the phone number of the older couple who had him.

"He's pretty young," Rick said, referring to the pony. "Only three or four, I think. But he's real honest and easy to get along with. They'd probably let him go pretty reasonable to a good home."

We had four months before the summer season started. I wasn't really looking to buy a pony that soon, but I figured if Rick was recommending this one, I should at least go have a look.

When I phoned, an older woman answered. I told her Rick had given me their number, and that I was calling about the pony they had for sale.

"You should probably talk to my husband," the kindly voice said. "He knows more about these things than I do."

Seconds later, her husband, Harold, came on the line. I asked him a few pertinent questions about the pony—how old he was, how long they had him, what they used him for, whether he had any bad habits, and lastly, how much they were selling him for.

Harold said they'd bought the pony as a long yearling for their grandson, who at the time was three years old. Over the three years they'd had him, they put the grandson on him once or twice a week, mostly on weekends when their son and his wife brought him by to visit, and just led him around the backyard. He said the pony was actually a miniature horse (not a real pony) that had grown a little too big to be shown in miniature horse shows. But now, not only was his grandson six years old and getting too big for the pony, but his son had taken a job in Maryland, so they only saw the grandson once or twice a year.

"He's just too nice of a horse to be standing around," Harold said. "So we're looking for a good home for him."

"I'd like to come have a look at him if I could," I said.

"Well," Harold's voice cracked over the phone, "if Rick gave you our number, he must think you'll give him a good home. I guess you'd better come on over."

I got the directions and set up a time three days later, on a Saturday morning, to go have a look. Back then, pretty much the only time we trailered horses anywhere was when we moved ten or so at a time from the ranch to winter pasture and back. As a result, we didn't have much need for a small trailer and, in fact, didn't even own one. The only trailer we had was a thirty-two-foot stock trailer we pulled with a one-ton dually Ford pickup. From what Harold had told me about the pony, I had a pretty good feeling I was going to want to take him home. So it was the big trailer I hooked up that Saturday morning when I went to take a look at the little horse.

Harold was a retired farmer living near Ft. Collins, and it wasn't hard to find his place, a well-kept old homestead on the edge of a town that was quickly closing in on him. I swung the rig into the yard and parked it so it would be easy to pull back out onto the road. Harold and his wife, Betty, met me as I climbed out of the cab.

We made our introductions and shook hands. Betty asked if I'd like some coffee, which I politely declined, never having developed a taste for the stuff.

"Well, then," Harold said, "let's go on back and have a look at him."

"Sounds good," I agreed.

"Now you know," Harold said, glancing at the enormous trailer as we walked past it, "miniature horses are pretty small."

"Yessir," I said, respectfully, "I know."

"And we've only got the one for sale."

"Yessir."

Like most folks who have spent their lives scratching out a living on the scrabble of the high plains, seeing waste of any kind just didn't sit right with them. Hauling one small horse in a rig designed to carry ten or twelve big ones was, I'm sure, the epitome of ostentatious waste in Harold's eyes, and it was clear he didn't like it.

I explained to him that even though this rig was way more than we needed to haul one small horse, it was the only one we had. I told him how I'd tried to borrow a smaller rig but just wasn't able to on short notice. I think my explanation made him feel a little better. After all, while waste of any kind certainly made him uncomfortable, he also understood about having to make do with what you had.

We walked down a path away from the house, around a small shed, and there in a pen just behind the shed was the pony, munching on a flake of nice-looking hay. He was a scruffy little thing less than three feet tall at the withers and dark sorrel in color, with a bushy main and tail that looked as though they wanted to turn flaxen. His forelock puffed out just above his eyes, and his thick winter coat made him look like he weighed about 100 pounds more than he did. Not really the prettiest pony I had ever seen.

Harold, Betty, and I visited some more about the little horse they had named Sam and how he had been nothing but a solid citizen ever since they bought him. He had no vices or bad habits, was easy to trim, saddle, lead, catch, and tie, and best of all, was good around little kids. Harold pulled a tiny saddle and pad from the shed and cinched the saddle to Sam's back without even putting a halter on him. We then haltered him and led him around some, which the pony did very willingly. I picked up all four of his feet, which he also allowed without any trouble.

"Now," Harold said. "I want you to know that he's packed our grandson around plenty, but always when someone was leading him around. And doing that, he's never offered to do a thing wrong. But he ain't never been rode by himself, and so I would have to say he probably ain't what I would call 'broke to ride.' I don't know what he'd do if someone just tried to ride him out."

"Well," I told him, "that shouldn't be a problem. All we want him for is pony rides anyway. I doubt anybody will ever just get on and ride him."

"I expect he'd be just the ticket, then," Harold nodded.

With that, I asked what Harold's price was, and he told me $225 including the saddle, pad, and halter. I easily talked him down to $200, which I think both of us fully expected I would at least try to do, and then I loaded the little guy in the huge trailer and took him back to the ranch.

Before leaving Harold and Betty's place, I called home to let my wife know I was bringing Sam home, and when I arrived at the ranch, Wendy was waiting by the barn with our three children—Lindsey, who was nine years old at the time; Tyler, who was six; and Aaron, who was five. No sooner had I unloaded the scruffy little pony than the three kids surrounded him and spent the next several minutes petting, hugging, and (in Lindsey's case) kissing him on his nose.

A few minutes later, I broke off the lavish welcome-home party and told the kids I needed to get Sam settled in his temporary home, the small catch pen out behind the barn made of a five-rail wooden fence. (Once again, a five-rail fence for a three-foot-tall pony was overkill, but it was all we had for him at the time.)

Wendy and Lindsey decided to go back up to the house, and the two boys stayed with me. Tyler led Sam through the gate and into the pen, as Aaron closed and secured the gate behind them. I filled a few water buckets and hung them low on the fence so Sam could reach them, and I got a few flakes of hay, which I put on the ground nearby.

The three of us stayed in the corral for several minutes watching Sam munch away, when Tyler, dressed in all his cowboy regalia—boots, hat, little Carhartt jacket, and chinks—asked if he could ride him. I explained to Tyler that we would give the pony a couple days to get comfortable with his new home before we did anything with him, and besides it was starting to get late and it would be supper time soon.

"I bet he wouldn't mind if I rode him," Tyler reasoned.

"Not today," I slowly shook my head.

"He looks like he wants someone to ride him, though," Tyler said, looking at his brother. "Don't he Aaron?"

Aaron, also wearing his cowboy hat, a hand-me-down from Tyler that was just a hair too big for him, nodded in agreement.

"Not today," I repeated.

I asked the boys if they wanted to help me unhook the trailer (knowing full well that hanging out with a new pony was way more fun than watching their dad unhook a trailer). They both graciously declined.

"Okay," I cautioned, just before heading over to the truck. "But don't bother the pony, okay? He's having his supper right now."

"We won't bother him," Tyler smiled.

"We won't baaver him," Aaron repeated.

"Promise?" I asked.

"We promise," Tyler nodded.

"Pwamiss," Aaron chimed in.

I left the boys in the corral with the pony, feeling confident they wouldn't terrorize the little guy, and went about my business of parking and unhooking the trailer. I had just about finished cranking the jack up high enough for the gooseneck of the trailer to clear the bed of the pickup when both boys came around the barn, laughing and giggling.

"What's so funny?" I asked, as they approached.

"Nothing," Tyler giggled.

"Noffing," Aaron chirped.

Both boys were still at an age where witnessing a horse's bodily functions in action was sometimes the funniest thing they ever saw, and I guess I just figured something like that had occurred behind the barn, and that was probably what they were laughing at.

"Okay," I smiled. "I'm just going to check on the pony one more time. Then we'll go up for supper."

Both boys just chuckled.

I was a little surprised that Tyler didn't ask to ride the pony over the next couple days, especially seeing how set he'd been on riding him the day he arrived. Because it had been snowing off and on for both days, I just figured he was waiting for better weather before he asked again, and to be honest I didn't really give it all that much thought. Besides, the pony was settling in nicely, and as soon as the weather got a little better, I was going to lead the boys around on him anyway.

Three days after I brought Sam to the ranch, we had some friends over for dinner. We were all sitting around the table, talking about this and that, when out of the blue, Aaron chimed in with a comment.

"Tywer wode the pony," he said matter-of-factly, as he scooped some green beans into his mouth with his fork.

The table went silent for a second as all eyes fell on Aaron.

"What?" Wendy asked.

Aaron was chewing his beans and waited until he could swallow some before he spoke again.

"Tywer wode the pony," he repeated, as if it were common knowledge.

"He did?" Wendy asked with a hint of surprise in her voice. "When?"

"The aver day," he said, scooping up some more beans.

Wendy looked at me as if I was supposed to know what he was taking about … but I didn't.

"You rode the pony?" I asked, turning my attention to Tyler.

By now he had shrunk down in his chair a little and, with a mischievous grin, was looking over at Aaron. The same grin slowly crossed Aaron's face, as if they were the keepers of some really good secret that only the two of them knew.

Slowly, Tyler began to nod his head yes.

"When did you do that?" I was curious.

"The other day," he said quietly.

For the life of me, I couldn't figure out when he would have had time to go ride the pony. It seemed to me for the past two days, either Wendy or I knew where all the kids were at all times, and as far as either one of us knew, he hadn't gone down to the barn. But the problem was, neither Tyler nor Aaron were ones to tell lies about such things, so I guessed he must have somehow gotten down there without us knowing about it.

"You actually got on his back?" I asked.

Tyler nodded sheepishly.

"Did you put a saddle on him?"

Tyler shook his head no.

"You rode him bareback?"

Tyler nodded again. Wendy threw a concerned look in my direction, as if to say, *The horses are your department. You're supposed to know about these things!*

"Did you put a bridle on him?" I asked.

"No." Tyler was still smiling. Aaron started to snicker.

"Did you put a halter on him?"

"No." Now both boys snickered.

"You rode him without a halter or saddle?"

"Yup."

"How did you get on him?"

"I climbed on the fence." He smiled as he looked at Aaron. "And Aaron chased the pony around till it got close. Then I jumped on."

"You just jumped on and rode him?" Wendy asked, looking more at me than him.

"Yup."

"Did you fall off?" I asked.

"Naw," he shrugged. "When I was done, Aaron chased him around and when he got close to the fence I grabbed it." He mimed the way he had reached up and grabbed one of the fence rails to dismount.

"And where was your father during all this?" Wendy asked, now with a hint of amusement in her voice.

Aaron, evidently not knowing how to explain I had been unhooking the trailer while all this was going on, reached up and, putting his two hands together, moved them in a circle to simulate me turning the crank of the trailer jack.

Now it all made sense. That was why the boys were giggling when they came around the barn that evening and also why Tyler hadn't asked to ride the pony over the past two days. After all, why bother? He already had.

As seriously as I could under the circumstances, I tried to explain why doing what they did wasn't such a good idea and that they shouldn't do it again—not just for their safety, but also for the pony's. There were smiles all around as both boys agreed they wouldn't … and as far as I know, they never did again.

♘   ♘

As we finished our dinner that night, I remember getting up from the table thinking about that scruffy little pony and how, even though he could have easily (and certainly understandably) done something to hurt my two boys that day, still, he chose not to.

It was then that I knew for sure that even though he wasn't the prettiest pony I'd ever seen, he was indeed exactly the one we were looking for.

CHAPTER 4

Dynamite Fencing

"Being as soft as you want to be is not always the same as being as soft as you can be."

I ran into Dwight down at the Wheel Bar one night and noticed he looked a little haggard. We got to talking, and it turned out he'd just started a pretty major fencing project out on the ranch where he was foreman. Turns out there was about a mile-long stretch along the road right in front of the home place that needed replacing, and for nearly a year he had been arguing with the ranch manager about what kind of fence they should put up.

The ranch manager, it turns out, was an ex-banker from Missouri, and he was adamant about wanting to put up a three-rail wooden fence. Dwight, on the other hand, wanted to put up a cross-buck fence. Evidently, back in Missouri, a fella can dig a hole and set a wooden fence post just about anywhere he likes because the ground is soft and they have good dirt there. Out here in the Rockies, however, digging holes and setting wooden posts isn't that easy. Pretty much anywhere a fella tries to dig, he's bound to hit solid rock only inches below the surface.

Dwight said his boss's argument for the three-rail fence was it would be cheaper because it used less wood. Dwight's argument was that although the cross-buck would use more wood, it was going to be cheaper to build because it would take considerably less time to put up.

Dwight did his best to convince the banker-turned-ranch-manager that the three-rail fence would take twice or maybe three times the time and effort that a cross-buck would. But in

29

the end, the boss is still the boss, and so on that particular day, Dwight had been out trying to dig postholes in solid rock. He started at eight that morning, quit at five in the afternoon, and had only been able to get two-and-a-half holes dug … and that had been in the *good* ground!

"I got everybody else out doin' other projects," he said, motioning to Marlin, the bartender, to bring him another beer, "so I'm stuck tryin' to set this fence by myself. A mile of damn fence, and I'll be lucky to get it done by December."

"I don't have much going on tomorrow," I said, in what must have been a weak moment. "I could come out and give you a hand, if you want."

"I don't know if there's any sense in both of us bein' miserable all day." He lit a cigarette. "But I wouldn't mind the help, if you feel like comin' by."

"No problem."

"Why don't you meet me at the Big Horn for breakfast," he said, taking a sip from his glass. "If nothing else, at least you'll get a full stomach out of the deal."

So, with that, my fate was sealed.

U U

Like most folks who've been around ranching for any amount of time, I've put up my share of fence. Every once in a while in this part of the West, if a guy is lucky, you might hit some good ground to dig in, and you can get seven or eight holes dug and posts planted in a day. But that ground up by Dwight's place wasn't good ground. In fact, the only good ground was the spot where Dwight had dug the day before. It got worse after that.

When Dwight and I got to the site, the tools he used the day before were still right where he'd left them. There was a John Deere tractor with a loader on the front and an auger on the back sitting next to the last hole he'd worked on. In the bucket were his hand tools: a posthole digger with the jaw tips bent and split from hitting rock, a spade shovel, and a six-foot-long, twenty-five-pound tamping rod, with a chisel point on one end for digging and splitting rock and a round "foot" on the other end used mostly for tamping dirt once the post was in the ground.

I checked the two holes Dwight had completed the day before and found them to be about two-and-a-half feet deep—the minimum depth for a good, solid, wood-rail fence. The third hole, the one he hadn't finished, was only about half that. That was the hole I would start on.

I knew it was going to be a long day when I thrust the chisel end of the tamping rod down into the hole in an attempt to break some of the rock loose, and all that happened was the rod bounced back up an inch or two and made a sound like a blacksmith's hammer hitting an anvil. Yessir, it was definitely going to be a long day.

It would take Dwight and me two-and-a-half hours to finish that hole and another four-and-a-half hours to dig the next one. We finished the day with a meager start on the third hole, even though it took us two hours to get that.

"That's enough of this foolishness," Dwight said, as we loaded the hand tools in the bucket of the tractor at the end of the day. "I'm gettin' a jackhammer tomorrow."

True to his word, the next day Dwight showed up with a pneumatic jackhammer from the rent-it place in town, and things did go a little smoother. By late afternoon we'd been able to finish the hole we hadn't finished the day before and punch six more good ones. On the third day, we were able to get about three holes dug in the morning, but then we ran into some ground that even the jackhammer couldn't get through. We tried to bust rock in one hole for several hours, and only got about six inches deeper than when we started.

The following day didn't go much better. By this time we had only gone about half the distance we needed to go to get all the posts in, and it appeared as though we weren't going to get any farther. The two of us had been struggling over one hole in particular for quite a while when Dwight went over and shut off the jackhammer.

"I'm goin' to town for a few minutes," he said, wiping the sweat from his brow. "You could go ahead and start putting posts in the holes we got finished, if you want."

I agreed. And with that, Dwight jumped in his pickup and headed for town, and I went back to where he'd started digging a couple days before. Nearby were several bundles of posts, each held together with metal bands. I went over to a bundle and popped the bands, causing the posts to roll out on the ground. I went about the business of putting a post in each of the holes we'd dug. When I'd used the last post, I popped another bundle of fourteen posts open and did the same thing with them.

Dwight was only gone for half an hour or so, and about the time he got back, I was placing posts in the holes closest to where we'd stopped before he left. Dwight jumped out of the truck, looked at the posts standing crooked in the holes (I hadn't set or leveled them, just put them in the holes), and nodded his approval.

"Do me a favor," he said, without waiting for a reply, "and go bring the tractor over here."

"Sure," I turned and headed for the tractor, nearly half a mile away.

I looked back occasionally and could see Dwight kneeling on the ground near the hole we were struggling with, but other than that didn't see anything out of the ordinary. But then, just as I reached the tractor, there was suddenly a tremendous explosion back where Dwight was working.

I instinctively ducked when the explosion rocked the ground, then immediately turned and looked back in Dwight's direction. At first all I could see was a huge cloud of dust rising in the air, and thinking that something real bad had happened to Dwight,

I started running in his direction. I hadn't gone but about twenty yards when out of the dust cloud came Dwight, running my way.

"Bring the tractor," he yelled, motioning me to go back. "We need the tractor down here!"

I turned in my tracks and hurried back to the tractor. Within minutes I'd driven it to where Dwight was, and I could see what had happened. The dust cloud had subsided some by then, and by the amount of rock and debris on the road and up in the grass, it was pretty clear Dwight had simply gone and blasted the area with dynamite. That's why he went to town. I knew he had a friend that dealt in the stuff and also knew he had used it in the past for blowing beaver dams and such. I just never would have thought to use it for fencing.

Well, I thought to myself, *we won't have too much trouble digging now.*

Dwight motioned for me to clean the rocks off the road with the tractor's front-end loader, and while I did that, he went down a little farther and set another charge. Within minutes there was another explosion, this one not as big as the first, and again I was cleaning rocks off the road. One more explosion after that and he had effectively loosened up enough ground that we could actually get the rest of the postholes dug and posts put in.

U U

As you can imagine, fencing over the next couple days went pretty smoothly. In the same time it took us to dig the first half of the fence line, we were able to dig the rest of the holes and also set the posts and hang the rails. The only problem was that now the ground was a little too soft, but we made do. The end result was a pretty nice-looking fence, if I do say so myself.

Over the years Dwight and I have reminisced a number of times about the day we did some "dynamite fencing," and each time we talk about it, we can't help smiling. A lot of years have passed since the two of us put up that fence. Since then Dwight has left the ranch and gone on to other things. And that ranch manager, well, he's gone, too.

The fence held up for a long time, but here recently I noticed it was starting to show its age and sections of it are slowly being replaced by the folks there at the ranch … with a nice, new cross-buck.

CHAPTER 5

Snow in July

"Never argue with the natural ignorance of a greenhorn."

I think everybody who works with horses should, at least once in their lives, get themselves a job at a dude ranch. Horse strings at dude ranches are a smorgasbord of equine personalities. Yessir, there is no question that you can learn a lot about horses at one of those places.

However, as much as a fella can learn about horses working a dude string—and that can be considerable—what can be even more interesting is getting a glimpse of the quirky personalities of some of the people who show up to ride. One such group of folks comes to mind whenever I get to thinking about those interesting trips into the mountains back when I was guiding dudes.

We'd just finished morning chores when the owner of the string, Steve Wilson, told me he needed me to take out a "private" all-day ride. Evidently, some rich folks from back east had paid a premium to ride up to Odessa Lake. Now, from the barn to the lake and back would be a good seven-hour round trip, providing we only stopped for lunch and maybe another time or two for a "bathroom" break. I had to wonder if this group would actually be up to it.

"Do these folks ride?" I inquired, hoping they did, but figuring they probably didn't. It had been my experience that folks who ride or own their own horses don't often ride dude strings when they're on vacation.

"Don't know," Steve shrugged. "They should be here in about fifteen minutes. Go on and get ready." He turned and started walking away. Almost as an afterthought he looked back over his shoulder. "Sack lunches are in the cook shack. There's one in there for you, too, if you want it. Ham, I think."

Some of my fellow wranglers didn't care much for taking out all-day rides. I could hardly blame them, I guess. If you didn't get the right group of riders behind you—and the group of riders you got was *always* a crapshoot—an all-day ride could end up being an awful lot of work. Even with good riders, the guide would often spend a lot of time stopping so folks could take pictures, or getting off his or her horse to pick up something that someone dropped, or getting everybody slickered up when it started raining, or finding good places for folks to stop and relieve themselves … and so on.

Still, I didn't mind the all-day rides too much. I'd taken out quite a few in my two years at this job, and overall they had been pretty pleasant trips. So I just went about my business getting ready for the trip and didn't think too much more about it.

I got my saddle bags and tied them to the back of my saddle. I made sure I had a first-aid kit, some matches, and a roll of toilet paper. It never failed on these long rides that folks, having been so excited about the trip itself, would forget about the fact that nature might, and often would, call when there just weren't any modern facilities anywhere within miles. There'd been more than one occasion when the roll of toilet paper stuffed down in the bottom of my saddle bags came in pretty handy for a "guest in distress."

I checked each of the sack lunches in the cook shack to make sure the contents hadn't been tampered with. It wasn't uncommon for one of the wranglers, as a practical joke, to sneak in the cook shack when nobody was looking and sabotage the guide's sack lunch. I've got to say, there was nothing more disheartening than being out on an all-day ride and stopping for lunch, only to find what you expected to be a ham sandwich was nothing more than two pieces of bread with a half-dozen sticks or twigs between them, or perhaps the excess hoof from the last round of shoeings, or maybe a spattering of pony manure ... or pretty much anything else handy that would make for a good joke when you went to take a bite of your sandwich.

With all the lunches passing inspection—a proper sandwich wrapped in cellophane, an apple, a bag of potato chips, and a chocolate chip cookie, also wrapped in cellophane—I took them out and placed them in my saddle bags as well. I checked all the horses we'd be taking to make sure shoes were tight, good slickers were tied to the backs of the saddles, and that everyone had a full canteen of water hung over the saddle horn and secured tightly with the saddle strings.

We would all be pretty well mounted for this trip, as any all-day ride would be. My horse was the same one I'd been guiding off of for the past two years, a big, black quarter horse named Roulette. Evidently, Roulette got his name years before because, as legend had it, getting on him was like playing Russian Roulette. You just never knew from one time to the next whether or not you were going to survive riding him. I guess somebody down the line must have rode all the rough off him, though, because he and I sure never had any trouble.

Once all the horses were checked and the saddlebags packed, I got myself ready. Even though it was midsummer, I still wore a long-sleeved shirt, with a T-shirt under that. I got my wool vest and my lined Carhartt jacket and put both of them on. Then I strapped on my chaps and tied an extra jacket on the back of my saddle, over the top of my slicker. I sharpened my knife and placed it back in its sheath on my belt, then took an old, worn pair of leather gloves and stuffed them in my belt as well. The last thing I did was tie my lariat to my saddle. Then I headed back up toward where the riders would be registering.

As I walked back toward the office, two of my fellow wranglers passed me heading the other direction. One was smiling, the other snickering a little.

"What's so funny?" I asked as they walked past.

"You'll see," one of them responded. With that, they burst out laughing.

I shrugged it off and went up to the office. When I got there, Steve was standing on the porch with what looked like four tourists, two men and two women, all dressed in tank tops, shorts, and sandals.

"Here he is," Steve said, as he saw me approach. "Mark, these are the folks here for the all-day ride."

He introduced me first to Don, a fella about five-nine, slightly overweight, with short, dark hair. The skin on his face, arms, hands, feet, and legs was pasty white, like that of the other three people he was with. They obviously didn't spend a whole lot of time outside. I was then introduced to Don's girlfriend, Carol. She was also about five-nine, wore glasses, was thin, and had medium-length, reddish hair.

"This is Audrey." I shook hands with a dark-haired gal about five-three, attractive, with three earrings in one ear, two in the other. Even though none of them were wearing a whole lot in the way of proper clothing, Audrey was wearing even less. Her shorts were real short, and her top—what there was of it— would have made Hugh Hefner blush.

"And this is Audrey's fiancé, Jeff."

Jeff was about six-feet tall, with short, dark hair and a close-cropped beard and moustache. We shook hands and I stepped back and stuffed my hands in my jacket pockets.

"Okay," I said matter-of-factly, "I'm ready to go when you are. I expect you'll want to change before we head out, though."

"Change?" Audrey scoffed. "Why?"

"You're going to be in the saddle for a long time today," Steve interjected. "Wearing shorts for a ride that long ... well, your legs'll look like hamburger by the time you get back."

"I thought we were just riding up to a lake or something," Audrey said. "It's a beautiful day, why would we want to change our clothes?"

"It's nice down here right now," I explained, "but the lake is up over 10,000 feet, and before we can get to it, we will be going above timberline, then dropping down to it. The weather can, and often does, change fast up there and it's just better to be prepared."

"I told you," Jeff said, looking down at Audrey. "Come on. Let's go put something else on."

"There's a restroom across the way," I said, pointing to the little log building across the road from the office. "You can change in there."

Don, Carol, and Jeff all started in the direction of their car, where they had a change of clothes, but hesitated when Audrey didn't move.

"I'm not changing," Audrey said, defiantly crossing her arms over her chest. "I came here to get some sun, and that's what I'm going to do."

"You'd be better off getting your sun laying by the pool at your hotel," Steve advised.

The look on Audrey's face told us she didn't agree.

"It's up to you, though … it's your backside," Steve looked down at her painted toenails protruding out of the $300 sandals on her feet. "Even if you don't want to put some jeans on, you're still going to have to change your shoes. We can't take you on a ride wearing sandals; our insurance won't let us."

"I didn't bring any other shoes with me," Audrey whined.

"Come on, Audrey," Carol motioned, as she and the others turned again toward their car. "I've got some tennis shoes that might fit you."

"Fine," Audrey grunted. "Whatever."

"Bring jackets if you have them," I said.

"We're from New York," Audrey said, glancing over her shoulder without stopping. "We know what cold is … and this isn't it. I think we'll be all right." She turned back around and got a little chuckle from her friends.

I figured it wasn't going to help to tell her it wasn't unusual in the mountains for the temperature to drop ten degrees for every thousand feet in elevation we would climb—and we were going to climb 3,000 feet before finally dropping down to Odessa Lake. With the temperature that morning at about 75 degrees, it wouldn't be out of the realm of possibility to have temperatures in the mid- to low-40s before we reached our destination. But, like she said, Audrey knew what cold was, so I figured there was no need for me to worry or argue.

About a half-hour later, the five of us—Jeff, Don, and Carol wearing their jeans, T-shirts, and tennis shoes, Audrey in her shorts, tank top, and tennis shoes, and myself—were mounted up and heading down the trail with Roulette and me in the lead.

Like most of the rides out of our livery, the one to Odessa Lake was extremely pretty. Well, I guess I should say most of the ride was pretty. The first hour or so was on a trail relatively close to the only road to Bear Lake, a popular tourist destination. The trail was on a south-facing moraine that sloped gradually down to the road. With the road so close, we saw and heard a lot of traffic for the first hour.

This part of the trail was flooded with sunlight and also fairly sheltered from the wind. As a result, the air felt probably ten or fifteen degrees warmer than it actually was. It was during this part of the ride that I had to endure Audrey's thinly veiled sarcasm.

"Wow," Audrey mocked at one point, "is it always this cold up here? Jeez, I hope I don't freeze to death!"

I have to admit, this part of the trail was warmer than I expected, and I had broken into a sweat under my Carhartt. Even so, I wasn't about to take it off.

After about forty-five minutes on the trail, the Bear Lake road curves south while the trail continues west and passes Hollowell Park. It's interesting that, in Colorado, mountain valleys are often referred to as "parks." For instance, the town I live in, Estes *Park*, is situated in a valley named after the first family to settle here.

Farther up north, in Wyoming, Idaho, and the like, valleys are referred to as "holes," as in Jackson *Hole*, Wyoming.

In any case, we were riding into Hollowell *Park* (or valley), which was surrounded by tall mountains. As valleys go, Hollowell isn't all that big, perhaps a half-mile square. We would ride through the valley and pick up the trail on the other side, as it ran along a small creek and up a narrow gulch. It was there we would begin the long, slow ascent that would eventually take us up above timberline.

From there on out, the trail would be shaded by tall ponderosa pines and the aspen trees that hadn't yet been choked out by old-growth forest ... and the temperature would slowly begin to drop.

Shortly after we entered the gulch, I suppose a little over an hour-and-a-half since we'd left the barn, the group began to quiet down some. Up to that point they'd been pretty chatty, making jokes, talking about this and that and the other thing, and taking the occasional pot shot at me for being overdressed on such a nice day.

For the most part I'd stayed pretty quiet, pointing out the occasional deer or elk and answering a few questions about local history that Don asked from time to time. I did mention how quickly the weather could change in the Rockies and that we needed to get up above timberline and back down into the trees before about two in the afternoon. I explained how storms often move in off the divide about that time of day and that we didn't want to get caught out in the open up there if we could help it.

Their comments made it pretty clear that they didn't believe me. With the exception of Carol, the group found my remarks about the possible weather change one more thing to make jokes about. Yet, while they were laughing, I kept my eye on the occasional wispy white clouds that were beginning to streak the sky above us.

We climbed the gulch, crossed a creek, and stopped in a small clearing for a much-needed break. I got everybody off their horses and, holding all the mounts, took a seat on a large rock in the grass. The four of them scurried off into the trees and bushes and returned a few minutes later looking a whole lot more "relieved."

I could tell by the way everyone was walking that they weren't used to being on horseback. As they came back, Don and Jeff cracked the usual jokes about now understanding why cowboys walk bowlegged and a few more jokes about being hungry but not seeing a McDonald's along the way.

While they were enjoying themselves, I was paying attention to those clouds overhead, the wispy ones that were beginning to get a little mass to them, along with a touch of gray. I also noticed Audrey's arms, face, shoulders, and the tops of her legs were starting to turn pink … a sure sign that someone has been in the high-mountain sun without sunscreen.

I mentioned to her that she was starting to burn a little and that I had some sunscreen in my first-aid kit if she needed it. She made some comment about me not being her mother and told me I needn't worry about her. I dropped the subject and never brought it up again.

Before long we were on our way again. About an hour or so later we passed high above Bear Lake, where we stopped so the group could take pictures. We continued our climb and before long the tall pines gave way to the smaller scrub-like evergreens of the subalpine tundra.

About this time the clouds I'd been watching had assembled in a dark mass over the divide, the area we were slowly closing in on, and were starting to roll ominously over the nearby peaks. The temperature had dropped a good twenty degrees since we left the barn, and while I was still pretty warm and comfortable, my charges were obviously becoming a little chilled, although none of them was bound to admit it.

We climbed higher and began to encounter small drifts of dirty snow left over from the winter months. At one point we had to ride through a thirty-foot swath that covered the trail and was deep enough in the middle the horses had to lunge forward to keep from getting stuck. It was about this time that I noticed the hard-line façade Audrey had presented all day was beginning to crack.

We were only a couple of miles from getting over the pass and dropping down to our destination, which was well below timberline and much less exposed. If we stopped at any point between here and there, we would certainly be in for trouble if the weather, which looked pretty nasty and appeared to be heading our way, moved in. Over the past hour or so Audrey had asked a number of times if we could take a break and get off for a while. Concerned about the group's safety, I kept them moving as long as I could, but after the horses lunged through the snow, Audrey had had enough and was almost begging to get off.

"Okay," I finally relented, watching the dark clouds roll toward us. "But just for a couple minutes. We really need to keep moving."

I got everybody off their horses and let them stretch their legs. By then it was almost impossible for them to hide the fact that they were all not only getting saddle sore, they were also getting pretty cold. Carol had been the only one to bring a jacket, and as soon as she was off her horse, she put it on. Jeff and Audrey huddled together as they took up a seat on a nearby fallen log, and Don, who was beginning to shiver some, asked if it would be all right for him to put his slicker on to help warm himself up.

I told him I thought that was a great idea and began pulling all the slickers off the saddles. Everybody quickly pulled their slickers on, with the exception of Audrey, who refused, complaining the old yellow raincoats smelled funny. I offered her my spare jacket, but she refused that as well.

By this time, Audrey's skin was so sunburned she was beginning to look like a boiled lobster, and the inside of her calves and thighs appeared to be rubbed raw from the saddle. I explained to her that if she wore her slicker (which was fleece-lined), not only would she be warmer, but she could wrap the lower part of the slicker around her legs, which might relieve some of her discomfort. She wasn't interested.

The rumble of distant thunder to the west cut our stop short. I got everybody mounted up as quickly as I could and got under-way. We continued up the trail, and as I watched, the peaks that loomed in front of us slowly began to disappear in a shroud of mist. *Here comes the rain,* I thought to myself.

Within minutes of leaving our resting spot, we also left the safety of the trees and became completely exposed to the ele-ments. It would be a mile or so before we would begin our de-scent to the lake. Above timberline I had an unobstructed view of the weather, and it was heading straight for us. The prospect of getting hit with any weather above timberline was worrisome enough, but as I got a clearer view of what was heading our way, my anxiety turned into all-out trepidation. I had just assumed we were in for a good, old-fashioned soaking. In reality, what was heading for us was a full-blown snow squall.

"Audrey," I said, turning in my saddle, "I really think you should put that slicker on."

I had tied her slicker loosely to the front of her saddle to make it easier for her to retrieve, should she change her mind about wearing it.

"I'm not wearing that smelly old thing!" she shouted back, a slight shiver in her voice.

"Come on, honey," Jeff pleaded. "You must be freezing. Hell, I'm cold and I've got mine on!"

"Just get us out of this godforsaken place," she yelled, looking right at me.

I turned back around in my saddle just in time to get hit in the face with a stinging, freezing rain. I urged Roulette forward, while untying my slicker from the back of my saddle and hur-riedly putting it on. Within seconds, the rain turned into sleet and then snow.

I stopped the group, dismounted, and ran back to Audrey, pulling the slicker from her saddle and trying to get it on her. Much to my surprise, she absolutely refused my efforts and actually screamed at me to leave her alone. I couldn't believe what I was seeing. There she was, burnt to a crisp from the sun, dressed only in a now-soaked tank top, shorts, and tennis shoes, in a snowstorm, refusing a raincoat.

I quickly decided rather than trying to fight with her about the slicker, my best plan of action would be to get all of us down below timberline as quickly as possible. With that, I jumped on Roulette and began trotting the group toward the canyon that would take us down to the lake. We had a good half-mile to go before we would reach the top of the pass, and we covered that ground in pretty good time. Once at the top of the pass, the trail made a curve to the right and began the gradual descent that would eventually take us back into the trees.

By the time we reached the curve, the visibility was next to nothing, and it was everything I could do to keep track of the third and fourth riders in the line, Audrey and Jeff. The good news was we were finally beginning our descent. The bad news was that we needed to slow down considerably because the trail narrowed greatly. On the right was a rock wall that turned into an overhang, and on the left there was about a thousand-foot drop-off. Basically, for about 200 yards we would be riding downhill on an exposed, narrow shelf far above Odessa Lake, which we couldn't see at the time because of the snow.

The first half of the traverse went pretty smooth, even though we were getting blasted by this freak summer snowstorm. Then, as luck would have it, the snow suddenly stopped … just like that. Now you might think that would be a good thing, and normally it would be … but not on this trip.

As the snow stopped, the canyon filled with the ear-piercing, panicked screams of one of my riders. A quick turn in my saddle revealed the screams were coming from none other than Miss

Audrey. Not only was she screaming at the top of her lungs, she was also doing everything she could to get down off her horse.

I stopped my horse and, as rapidly as I could, made my way back to her along the narrow edge of the trail between the horses and the drop-off. I reached her just in time to push her back into the saddle.

"Audrey!" I tried to raise my voice above her screams. "Audrey! What's wrong?"

She looked like a drowned rat. Her hair was covered in melting snow and clung to her face, her clothes were soaked, her fingers were wrinkled like prunes, and she was covered in goosebumps. But the one thing that really got my attention was that the color of the skin on her arms and legs, which only minutes before had been beet-red, was now almost as white as a sheet. Then I noticed her lips were an odd shade of blue.

"E f'aid mm hats," she yelled in a quavering voice that didn't sound at all like hers. "It ee gown!"

She fought against me, trying to get off her horse.

"Audrey," I pushed her back up. "I don't understand what you're saying."

"E f'aid mm hats," she started sobbing. It was obvious she was so cold she was having trouble forming her words properly. "It eeeee gown! It eeee gown!"

"Oh, crap," Jeff suddenly interjected. "She's afraid of heights! I forgot all about that!"

Her head started nodding almost uncontrollably. When the snow was falling, the visibility had been so bad she wasn't able to see how high up she was above the canyon floor. Once the snow stopped and she could see into the depths, she panicked.

"She wants to get off," he explained. "She's saying she wants to get off."

"She can't," I said to Jeff, then turned back to Audrey. "You can't get off. It's too dangerous. We're almost to the trees. Another

100 yards and we'll be away from this edge. You have to stay on your horse; you can't get off."

"Ont it gown," she sobbed, her head dropping to her chest, her teeth chattering.

"Everything's okay," Carol said, reassuringly. "That horse doesn't want to go off the edge any more than you do."

"That's right," I agreed, starting back toward Roulette. "Stay on your horse, Audrey. I'm going to get us down as quick as I can. You stay on."

I mounted up quickly, keeping a close eye on Audrey. As soon as we moved, she once again started her blood-curdling screams. This time I didn't stop. I kept pushing forward, figuring she wouldn't try to get off a moving horse, and she didn't. Before long we reached timberline. We pushed on to the lake where we would normally have stopped for lunch, but about that time, a cold rain began to fall again.

Everybody was wet and cold, but Audrey was by far the worst of the bunch. I was afraid if I got her off her horse, I might not be able to get her back on. So rather than stopping at Odessa Lake, as was the plan, I made the decision to push on to Fern Lake, another half hour or so down the trail. There was good shelter near the lake, and if for some reason Audrey wouldn't be able to ride again once we got her off, it was only about forty-five minutes to the nearest help down in Moraine Park.

Once off the ledge, Audrey, as well as the rest of the group, became very quiet. It continued to rain intermittently, but we arrived at Fern Lake safe and sound after about a half-hour. Just beyond the lake was a small clearing with a hitch rail next to the trail. Nearby there was a large boulder with a natural over-hang large enough for all the riders to get out of the rain for a while and have a little lunch.

As we arrived at the hitch rail, Carol, Don, and Jeff dismounted, and I immediately went to Audrey to help her down. Her movement was stiff and disjointed, her speech slurred and incoherent. She had stopped shivering, and her lips were blue and her skin pale. These were all signs of hypothermia, a life-threatening drop of core body temperature. The other three riders immediately came to Audrey's side as I eased her down on a nearby rock.

"I'm going to start a fire under that overhang," I told the group. "We've got to get her out of those wet clothes and wrapped in a couple of these slickers."

"Oh, no," Jeff said suspiciously. "She doesn't want to be naked around all you guys."

I didn't have time to argue. Audrey was fading fast, and if we didn't get her warmed up in a hurry, there was no telling how bad this was going to turn out. I immediately went about the business of finding some dry kindling, which I luckily discovered under the low branches of a spruce tree, along with a bit more from under the overhang. I brought some of the toilet paper from my saddlebags, stacked the kindling along with some dried pine needles just so, and placed a big wad of the paper under it. I struck a match to it. Before long we had a nice little fire going, and I continued to feed it for the next few minutes with a few larger sticks I had found nearby. Although the sticks smoked quite a bit due to their dampness, they made a warm fire nonetheless.

We placed Audrey next to the fire. After considerable urging, Jeff finally allowed Carol to disrobe Audrey behind a couple slickers he and Don held up as a makeshift blind. Carol then wrapped Audrey in her dry jacket, the one Carol had been wearing the entire time, and covered her with two slickers. The natural shelter of the overhang held in the heat very well. Coupled with the fact it had stopped raining and the sun was actually trying to come back out, things were beginning to look up.

About an hour later, with everybody dry and fed, the sun shining in a bright-blue sky, and Audrey having made nearly a full recovery and once again clothed, I extinguished the fire with water from the lake and covered it with three or four inches of dirt. We mounted up and finished the final leg of our trip. Other than a few grunts and groans from the riders being saddle sore, virtually no words were spoken by anyone the rest of the way.

Once we arrived back at the barn, some of the other wranglers helped the riders off their horses. When asked how they liked their ride, all of them, with the exception of Carol, responded by saying it was the worst experience they had ever had, anywhere. They said they would certainly never come back and wouldn't have gone in the first place if someone would have told them how cold it could get up there. Audrey jumped in, saying that she felt I should be fired for not making sure she had taken the proper clothing for the kind of weather they experienced.

♘ ♘

Exhausted, I led Roulette over to his pen and began taking the provisions out of the saddlebags. I got as far as the first-aid kit, then put it back and decided to just take the saddlebags off and carry them to the barn. I was untying the strings when I heard my name called. I turned around, and standing behind me was Carol. She reached out and shook my hand.

"I live in New York now," she smiled, as she held onto my hand, "but I grew up on a ranch up in the Bighorns. I know what you did for us up there, and I just wanted you to know, I appreciate it."

"Thank you for saying so." I was a little taken aback.

"They appreciate it, too," she nodded her head in the direction of her friends. "They just don't know it yet."

"I'm just sorry about Audrey ..."

"You know," Carol said, as she slowly released my hand, leaving something behind as she did, "my father always used to tell me, 'Never argue with the natural ignorance of a greenhorn, because in the end it's too much like trying to teach a pig to sing.'" She smiled. "You ever try to teach a pig to sing?"

"No." I smiled back.

"Well, don't. It'll only waste your time, and it aggravates the pig."

With that, she turned and walked back to her friends. As she did, I glanced into my hand to find she'd placed a $100 bill there.

Yessir … you can sure learn a lot about human nature working at a dude ranch.

CHAPTER 6

Wendy and the Draft Horse Baby

"Find a way to make a connection."

Dwight went up to Minnesota and bought four real nice Belgian mares from a friend of his, all of which were due to foal within the month. Two of the mares were for our friend Steve and the other two were for the ranch where I was foreman.

Even though I was foreman, we didn't live on the ranch at that time. Instead, Wendy and I had a little place outside of town with some land and a good-sized pen with a shelter up by the house. Dwight brought all four mares to our place where, we'd decided, we would foal them out. After the babies were born, Steve would pick up his mares and foals, and we'd move the other mares and their babies up to the ranch.

The mares arrived without fanfare and settled in quickly. They were pretty much the same size, about 16.3 hands and around 1,900 pounds, with the exception of one, a big mare named Mary that pushed eighteen hands and went a good 2,300 pounds. Having come from the same place, they were all easy going and got along together very well, so there was no need to separate them. Instead, we decided they'd all live together in the big pen. After they foaled, we'd separate them into a smaller pen only for a day or two until the babies could get their legs under them and then put them all back together again.

Two of the four mares really stood out for us during their stay, but for completely different reasons. The first was Jill. She was a very kind-hearted girl that was always the first to come up and say hello whenever someone went in to feed or clean the pen. But that wasn't really the reason she stood out.

For me, Jill was special because of the bond she seemed to form with Wendy. Within a matter of days, whenever Wendy entered the pen, Jill followed her around like a puppy dog, almost begging to be petted or scratched—and Wendy was always happy to oblige.

In the days leading up to the birth of Jill's foal, when she was about as big as a house and just about as uncomfortable as she could be, it was not uncommon for her to seek Wendy out and stand with her massive head leaning softly on Wendy's chest, the mare's eyes half closed and her breathing somewhat labored.

The second mare that stood out for us was Mary—not for her massive size, which was indeed impressive, but rather for her attitude toward us and toward her baby once it was born. Mary was the third of the four mares to have her foal, and being a maiden mare, she showed great interest in the two babies born before hers. However, when it came time for *her* to be a mother, all that changed.

U U

The weather was pretty nice for the end of April, and we got lucky on the nights the first two babies were born. While it had been somewhat chilly, the weather was dry and the births were uneventful. That was not to be the case with Mary.

Since she'd arrived and particularly following the first two births, Mary had appeared to go into labor on several occasions. But then, as if she simply willed it to happen, the labor would just stop. However, even *she* wasn't going to be able to hold back a baby that really wanted to come out.

We had been monitoring the weather over the past couple days, keeping an eye on a cold front that was scheduled to come through, carrying with it some moisture, probably in the form of snow. The day itself was very mild and pleasant, particularly for the first part of May in the mountains, but as evening fell, the wind shifted and a light breeze came out of the northeast. Along with it came the cold, damp air we were expecting, and we knew the snow wouldn't be far behind.

Along about seven in the evening Mary started acting a little uncomfortable, kicking and biting at her belly and occasionally laying down, flattening herself out on her side, then getting back up. Now, as I said, we had seen her do this on several occasions in the past few weeks, only to have it be a false alarm. But this time it really looked as though she might be serious, so we kept a very close eye on her as the night progressed.

Mary's symptoms came and went for the next three hours, and about ten o'clock, we decided to go to bed. I set the alarm to wake me about midnight so I could check on her. When I did, I could see the baby was determined to arrive, and in fact, his nose and front feet were already exposed, as Mary stood out in the pen looking more than a little annoyed.

We always tried to leave the brood mares alone when they gave birth and didn't get involved unless absolutely necessary. As I watched Mary over the next few minutes, I could tell this was going to be one of those times when we were going to get involved. She was walking around a bit and then almost throwing herself on the ground, which forced a little more of the foal to be exposed. She strained with the contractions that followed, but didn't seem to be able to make much progress. She would lay on the ground a little longer, then get back up, with the baby's front legs and nose exposed.

Wendy and I, along with my brother, Scott, who was living in our downstairs apartment at the time, went out to see if we could help her. She walked around a little and then, like before, sort of threw herself on the ground. This time when she started to have contractions, Scott and I each took one of the foal's front feet and pulled in time with the contractions in an effort to help Mary with her delivery.

Just then, it began snowing. First the flakes came down in a soft, light dusting. But the flakes soon grew in size and weight, carrying with them the moisture we'd been promised by the weatherman the previous day.

Our first attempt at freeing the foal was unsuccessful, although we did seem to make a little progress. Impatient with the results, however, the mare stood up again and walked around. Very quickly heavy wet snow was covering the ground, and where it wasn't melting and turning the dirt to mud, it was collecting in large white blotches where the ground was still frozen from the winter months.

I slid the mare's halter over her head and had Wendy hold the lead rope, not so much to try to stop her from moving, but to help her stay under control should she decide to leave the scene altogether. A few minutes passed, and the big mare once again tossed herself on the ground. Immediately, Scott and I took hold of the foal's front feet and began pulling each time the mare had a contraction.

We had a growing sense of urgency. The weather was worsening, the footing was bad, and the longer this went on, the more trouble both the mare and baby could get into. Scott and I pulled for all we were worth on each contraction, and even though it felt like we were pulling a '59 Buick up a hill with its parking brake on, this time our efforts began to pay off.

On about our third pull, the foal's head and some of his neck were exposed. On the next pull, his front legs and shoulders cleared the birth canal. At this point, the hard part for the mare appeared to be over, and with a few more pushes from her and pulls from us, the foal finally made his debut into the world.

The reason for the mare's trouble was immediately apparent. The colt was enormous! Now, of course, draft horse foals are always bigger than, say, the typical saddle horse foal. But even for a draft horse, this guy was huge.

Once the colt was on the ground, the mare seemed to relax, lying on her side and catching her breath. The baby was trying to lift his massive head and blow some of the mucus from his nose. After a couple of weak snorts, he made his first attempt at a whinny, which immediately got Mary's attention. She rolled up, sliding her legs under her, and turned her head in the direction of her baby. She nickered in answer, which prompted a little louder whinny from the baby and his first attempt to get to his feet—which failed miserably.

The mare let out another nicker and then, sliding a little on the muddy ground, pushed herself to her feet. Without shaking herself off, she turned and came around to her new foal. She put her head down, smelled him all over, and then began licking him.

Knowing this was the beginning of the natural bonding process between them, we backed away to let it progress. Much to our surprise, however, within minutes of their first contact, the mare appeared to lose interest in her new bundle of joy, and as if nothing had happened, she simply walked away from the baby.

It was still snowing pretty good, and the temperature had dropped considerably since the ordeal began. At that point, our main concern was getting the colt as dry as we could, as quickly as we could. Then we'd get him to his feet and put the two of them in the shelter, out of the weather. Wendy brought some old towels, and she and Scott began drying off the colt. While they were doing that, I brought Mary back to her baby, but she didn't appear to be interested in him at all.

We kept Mary near the colt as we finished drying him off and while he worked at standing up for the first time, which was no small feat in and of itself. It seemed to take a little longer than normal for the big colt to coordinate enough to get those extremely long legs under that very big body. Once he did, it seemed to take even longer for him to figure out how the legs worked.

Eventually, he was on his feet and sort of staggering around as best he could, looking for his mother and something to eat.

The only spark of interest Mary showed in the colt was when she pushed him away each time he got close to her. We moved the two of them to the shelter and closed them in.

Mary didn't seem too happy with this new arrangement. It surprised us to see the indifference Mary had for her baby, especially since most of the brood mares we had worked with over the years had been pretty good mothers and just instinctively took to the job. Maybe she thought her duties were finished once he was on the ground, or maybe she was holding a grudge for all the effort she had to expend just to get him there. Either way, it was clear she would much rather have been somewhere else on that cold, wet night.

Regardless, we continued to work on guiding the colt to Mary's flank while we asked her to stand still long enough for him to get there. You would have thought we were trying to dock two space shuttles, as much as the two of them struggled. Still, after a number of failed attempts, we finally got them together.

Then the next problem surfaced. The colt was so tall (and, needless to say, inexperienced at nursing) that he couldn't find a way to get to his mother's udder to nurse! Each time he tried, the best he could do was hit Mary on the flank with his nose, and as you can imagine, that didn't set too well with her. I worked with the baby for quite a while, trying to get him to drop his head low enough to get under her flank instead of *on* her flank. Eventually he did find the mark and got his first good meal out of the way, much to the annoyance of his mother. With that, we turned in for the night.

U U

Early the next morning the cold front had pushed through, and the day started out sunny and warm. We let Mary and her colt out of the shelter but noticed right away that he was no better at nursing than he had been the night before. Whenever he tried, he still hit Mary on the flank, and for her part, she was spending an awful lot of time pushing him away, although she did seem marginally more tolerant of him.

It was clear we needed to do something quickly to get some milk in the big colt, and I worked on getting him to drop his head again, as I had the night before. That morning, however, he was considerably stronger and more determined not to move his head that low. After slowly working with him for several minutes, it became clear we were going to have to go to plan "B"—milking the mare and feeding the colt with a bottle until he could figure out how to feed himself.

When I mentioned the idea to Wendy, she disappeared into the house and returned a short time later with two baby bottles she still had from when our kids were little. I had Wendy hold Mary while I went to the mare's flank and eased my hand down to her teat. Not surprisingly, by this time Mary had had just about enough of having her flank messed with, and she didn't seem at all happy with the idea.

Even though it was touch-and-go at times as to whether or not she was going to kick me, I was able to get the small bottle about half full of milk. Wendy placed a nipple on the bottle and cut a larger hole in the tip so the milk would flow easily. She offered it to the little guy, and he ate like it was going to be his last meal.

We had successfully gotten some milk into the colt, but we knew this was just the start. Not only were we probably going to have to milk Mary a number of times over the next few days, we also had to find a way to get this massive colt to lower his head enough to nurse on his own. On top of all that, we still had a mare that wasn't at all sure she wanted to be a part of the process.

It was clear we were going to need to get more milk from the mare each time we milked her. If we could get more milk into him at each feeding, hopefully we wouldn't have to feed him so frequently. We were also going to need a bigger bottle and nipple. While the little bottle worked all right, it just wasn't going to hold up under that heavy duty "sucker" the colt had.

I called our vet to see if he had a bottle for hand-feeding calves, which he did, and I drove over to his office to pick it up. By the time I got home, Wendy was feeding the colt again with the small bottle. She had somehow been able to milk the mare by herself, without tying her up or having anybody hold her. I found this a little surprising, seeing as thirty minutes before, the mare seemed perfectly willing to consider taking a shot at me with a hind leg when I milked her.

Even after finishing the bottle Wendy gave him, it was clear the baby was still hungry, so it was time to go back to milking the mare. I respectfully approached Mary with the newer, bigger bottle and eased my way down to her udder. As if on cue, she walked away, not wanting to have anything to do with the idea. Once she stopped I tried again, with exactly the same result.

About then, Wendy came over, took the bottle from me, walked over to Mary, and milked her just as easy as you please. The mare seemed perfectly happy to stand there and allow Wendy to do something she wouldn't even allow me to try. I looked over at Wendy.

"It's a girl thing," she said with a shrug.

It must have been, because for the next day-and-a-half, the mare let Wendy milk her pretty much anytime, day or night, without being restrained in any way. Each time I came around with that bottle, she protested in various ways, all of which told me just to let Wendy handle it.

After encouraging the colt to nurse using the big bottle, Wendy began moving the bottle closer to the mare's flank whenever she fed him. Eventually, she lowered the bottle down below Mary's flank, then under her flank, and after a couple of days the colt was able to find the mare's udder on his own (even though he needed to sort of squat down some to do it).

That's about the time Mary seemed to start warming up to the idea of being a mom. She not only began to allow the colt to nurse, but she also let him just hang out by her side like the other moms did with their foals, an achievement that had seemed nearly impossible just a couple days before. From that point forward, Mary became a model mother to her colt, and that behavior continued when they were moved up to the ranch a couple of weeks later.

By the time the colt was eighteen months old, he was already well over sixteen hands and weighed nearly 1,500 pounds. I started him in harness about that time, letting him pull very light loads hooked with his mother. I also hooked him with another older mare from time to time, one we occasionally used to help start our draft horse babies.

Eventually the colt became a really good pulling horse, and we used him and one of his half-sisters born the same year as a team on the ranch. By the time I left the ranch several years later, the colt had grown in size to nearly eighteen hands and well over 2,000 pounds.

I heard through the grapevine that the folks at the ranch had sold all their draft horses, including the colt, as well as the wagons and equipment associated with them. The last I heard, the colt had been sold to another ranch where he was used to pull hayrides for a couple of years. Then he was sold and used for quite a while as a carriage horse in Denver, and finally he went to a fellow who was using him as one of his wheel horses in a six-up hitch.

I find it interesting, the life that colt has gone on to live and the things he has done over the years. And to think, it all started so unceremoniously in our backyard, one cold and snowy evening.

CHAPTER 7

Diamond and Anne

"Horses remember everything that's important to them."

It was the first year that the guest ranch offered winter sleigh rides. Understandably, management wasn't real inclined to hire someone to help me with the rides until they saw what kind of interest there'd be in them. After all, there was no sense in having two people doing a job that one person could handle.

I had spent most of that fall building beds for the two twelve-person sleighs we'd be using (one main sleigh and one spare in case of a breakdown), as well as widening a path through the woods on the ranch to accommodate the sleigh and the team of draft horses that would pull it. The bed I built fit easily on top of the large, heavy bobsleds Dwight and I had bought at an auction the previous spring. By the time the first good snow fell in early November, both the trail and sleigh were more than ready to go.

When we got that first heavy snow, we loaded all of the ranch's department managers in the festively painted wooden box (on which I'd fastened old school bus seats scavenged from a junkyard) and headed out on our maiden voyage through the woods. After the ride, all the managers agreed we had a winner on our hands with our new sleigh-ride business. All we needed was customers.

With a big advertising blitz along the Colorado Front Range, we soon had more takers for sleigh rides than we knew what to do with. It was evident that not only would I need an assistant to help with the fledgling business, but we were also going to need an additional team of horses, as the work load from just a few weeks of rides was already beginning to wear down our only team.

With no time to waste, I made some phone calls and within a few days found a great team of Belgian draft horses named Diamond and Andy. Andy was of average size for a Belgian, about 17.2 hands and 2,200 pounds, but Diamond was massive—18.1 hands and 2,600 pounds. Together they made a formidable team, one that had no trouble pulling the big sled.

Then it was off to find an assistant to help with the rides. We put a few ads in local papers and agricultural weeklies but didn't get many calls from folks looking to work outdoors in the freezing-cold weather and spend all day looking at the south ends of northbound horses. Just when I was getting ready to give up on finding someone, a most unlikely candidate showed up.

♘ ♘

Like most guest ranches, there were a number of different departments on the place. There was the front desk, housekeeping, maintenance, food and beverage, conference services, and my department, the livery. But this ranch also had one more department, the health club.

Three or four full-time staff members and a handful of part-time staff worked at the guest ranch health club. One of these part-timers was a very petite young gal named Anne. Anne wasn't more than about five feet tall and couldn't have weighed more than 100 pounds soaking wet. I'd seen her around a few times, but because our schedules didn't match up, I'd never had a chance to meet her.

It was Saturday morning, and I was getting the team ready for a long day of sleigh rides. The first one was scheduled for 11:00 A.M. and the last for 9:00 P.M. The rides were pretty much back to back, and with only a fifteen-minute break between each ride, I wouldn't have much time for anything else.

I was leading the horses to the barn to feed, groom, and harness them when I saw Anne walking down the short road to the barn from the nearby health club building. Not thinking much of it, I just went about my business and put the big horses in the tie stalls with their morning grain. I was grooming Andy when I heard Anne's voice.

"Hello?" she called, loud enough for anybody who was in the barn to hear.

"Hello," I answered back.

"I'm looking for Mark," she said.

"That's me," I said, still brushing the immense surface area of Andy's body.

"I'm Anne," she called into the barn. "I work at the health club here on the property. I heard you're looking for help doing the sleigh rides."

"I am," I told her, stepping out from behind Andy's huge rear end and moving to his other side to continue grooming.

"I'll do it," she said, as if it were a foregone conclusion she'd get the job.

Somewhat amused by her confidence, I stepped out from behind Andy and went to the big door at the front of the barn where she was standing.

"Have you had any experience with horses?" I asked, as I opened the door and let her in.

"I've done some trail riding," she said, as she stepped inside the barn, "but that's about it."

As you might guess, I was not planning to hire someone with virtually no horse experience to help with the sleigh rides. In fact, I would have preferred someone with experience driving a team, but if they had at least some kind of horse background, I could teach them the basics relatively quickly. But this little waif of a girl, with no experience at all … well, to be honest, I pretty much dismissed her as a serious candidate out of hand.

Now most folks who haven't spent much time around horses are intimidated by the sheer size of even the average draft horse.

I figured pretty quick that all I'd need to do to discourage Anne from wanting the job was to get her right up next to one of those big guys, so I did.

Anne followed me back to the tie stalls. Andy had just finished his grain, so I went in and started backing him, because there simply wasn't any room in the stall for me to get in beside him and get him harnessed.

"This is Andy," I said, as I slowly backed him out.

"Wow," she almost gasped. "He's huge."

"So why do you want this job?" I asked as nonchalantly as possible.

"I need more hours," she replied, "and this time of year there aren't any extra hours available in the health club." She paused. "I don't know if I've ever seen a horse this big before."

"Come with me," I motioned for her to follow me as I made my way into the harness room. There, on two large hangers on the wall, were four sets of harness all neatly put away. Next to each was the collar that went along with that particular set of harness. Above each set was a small plaque with a horse's name.

I pulled Andy's collar down and headed back. I undid Andy's lead rope, slid the collar over his head and neck, and re-hooked the lead rope. As I did, I explained the proper way the collar went on the horse and what its function was. Then I went back in the harness room with Anne following close behind.

Each harness had been put on the hanger in such a way as to make it as easy as possible to remove and place back on the horse. The britchen—part of the harness that goes over the horse's hindquarters—comes off the hanger first and is placed on your shoulder. Then you lift the part of the harness known as the belly band off the hanger and place it in the crook of your arm. Finally you take a hame—one of the metal pieces that fit into the collar—in each hand and pull them from the hanger.

Good harness for these big horses is relatively heavy, often weighing around forty or fifty pounds, and it's all carried on one arm. It's also bulky and difficult to carry, even when done in the way I've just described. But the most difficult part for most people is getting the harness up on the horse. Lucky for me, I had harnessed enough horses over the years and was also tall enough and strong enough that throwing harness was probably easier for me than it is for most, and certainly easier than it would be for someone Anne's size.

I carried the harness over to Andy and eased it up on his back, dropping the hames over the collar, the belly band over his back and barrel, and the britchen over his hindquarters. I then set to connecting all the straps and buckles that held the harness in place, again explaining every detail to Anne as I went.

"Okay," I said, stepping away from the now-harnessed Andy. "Do you think you could do that by yourself?"

"I think so," Anne nodded. "Seems like it looks more complicated than it really is."

She was right. Most folks who harness a horse for the first time are overwhelmed by all the buckles, snaps, and leather. But once you look at how the harness is laid out on the horse and how it is held together, all the buckles, snaps, and leather make pretty good sense.

"Okay," I told her. "I've got to go up and clean the snow off the sleigh. If you can get that other horse harnessed by yourself by the time I get back, you got the job."

Now, bear in mind that Anne had not yet seen Diamond's full size. He was standing in the tie stall next to Andy, but there was a five-and-a-half-foot wooden wall separating them. That, coupled with the fact Anne had been paying so much attention to what I'd been doing while harnessing Andy that she never really even looked over at Diamond's stall, made me think she hadn't gotten a good look at him yet.

"Sounds good," she said and shrugged. With that, I left the barn and headed up the hill to the sleigh. It had snowed a little during the night, and all I needed to do was take a broom and brush the light dusting off the seats and floor, which didn't take more than about ten minutes.

I'm not sure what I expected to see when I got back to the barn, but one thing was certain … I sure didn't expect to find a harness on Diamond, which was the only reason I told Anne I'd hire her if she could harness him by herself. So you can imagine my utter amazement when I walked in to find not only the harness on Diamond's back, but everything on the harness buckled and snapped properly in place.

Anne was standing at Diamond's side, double-checking her work when I walked in.

"I had to stand on a bucket," she said, turning to me as I approached, "but I think everything is where it's supposed to be. You should probably check it, though." She turned back and looked at Diamond. "He seems a lot bigger than Andy."

♘   ♘

True to my word, I hired Anne on the spot and she started her duties as my assistant that day. She was a very hard worker who never complained once about the long hours or the oftentimes bitter cold we endured for hours on end. She was never late to work and never asked to leave early, and she had a great sense of humor, a very valuable asset when you spend a lot of time working in the cold and snow.

Over time, Anne became so comfortable in the job that I couldn't help but expand her duties from just harnessing the team, tending the horses, and helping with the rides, to having her spend some time now and then driving the teams. Like everything else she did, Anne took to being a teamster as though she'd been doing it all her life. She became so skilled that on a couple of occasions when we were so busy we needed to run two teams and sleds, I had no qualms about having her handle one team by herself, while I took the other.

As that first sleigh-ride season neared its end, I noticed something interesting. Diamond seemed to have developed a crush on Anne. Every time he saw her walking down to the barn, he ran to the fence of his pen and whinnied like he had found his long-lost mother.

In fact, he also learned to recognize the sound of Anne's little yellow Subaru. With the health club only a hundred yards or so from the barn, she parked her car in a nearby parking lot. I always knew when she got to work—whether she was working the sleigh rides or the health club—by the way Diamond announced her arrival. Often Anne would make her way down to his pen, even when she wasn't working the sleigh rides, just to give him a pat on the head. He seemed to enjoy that.

The sleigh-ride season ended. Soon the summer trail-ride season began with our saddle horses, and the draft horses went to work on hayrides. Still, Diamond remained vigilant for Anne's little Subaru, even though she spent less and less time at the barn and more time with her job at the health club.

The summer passed, and soon it was sleigh-ride season once again. All summer long Diamond had worked well in harness, very businesslike and tolerant of the guests who invariably wanted their pictures taken next to him. But as soon as the sleigh rides began and Anne started coming around again, his whole demeanor changed. He worked just as hard in harness, but his step seemed just a little higher, he seemed to pull just a little harder, and he was always just a little lighter in the lines.

We had another very busy season, and Anne began spending more time with her hands on the lines. She continued to improve as a teamster, and eventually I taught her how to drive the four-up, which she learned to handle very skillfully. As for Diamond, well, he continued to announce Anne's arrival on the property every day, but even more interesting, he began announcing her departures as well.

A few months after the end of our second sleigh-ride season, Anne told me she'd been hired on as a teacher in our local school district and, as a result, would have to resign her position at the health club and, sadly, as my assistant.

Several weeks later, after a great farewell party in the guest ranch's bar, Anne left the ranch for the last time. For weeks, Diamond spent hours at a time standing in the corner of his pen where he had a view of the health club parking lot. On a couple of occasions when he heard a car that sounded like Anne's, he'd run to the fence and nicker, only to walk disappointedly back to his feed bin a few minutes later.

When sleigh-ride season began, Diamond renewed his vigilant watch on the health club parking lot. But after a few weeks he seemed finally to come to the realization that Anne wasn't coming back and apparently gave up hope once and for all.

♘   ♘

Like always, Diamond worked well all season long and continued to do so into the following summer season. Anne seemed to fade from his memory, and he no longer went to the fence looking for her or listening for vehicles that sounded like hers. Even I lost track of Anne over time, having last heard she left her job as a teacher and took a position as a paramedic with the hospital.

I suppose a couple of years had passed when one day I was filling a water trough in Diamond and Andy's pen. Suddenly, Diamond's head shot up from his feeder full of hay and whipped around in the direction of the health club. He watched intently for a few seconds, ears pricked up and eyes focused forward. Then, with a little spring in his step, he slowly began trotting over to the fence. About halfway there he let out a loud, long whinny and shook his head three or four times. When he reached the fence, he let out another whinny and shook his head again.

A few seconds later, Anne came walking down the road. "Hey, big guy," Anne yelled.

Diamond whinnied and shook his head again and then trotted in a small circle and went right back to the fence.

I shut the water off while Anne made her way down to Diamond's pen. As she got to the three-rail wooden fence, Diamond hung his massive head over, and Anne reached up and stroked him between his eyes.

"I think he missed you," I said, giving Anne a little hug.

"I miss him, too," she said, hugging me with one arm and petting Diamond at the same time.

Anne hung out at the barn for an hour or so, and we caught up on all the pertinent news, told a few jokes, and reminisced about our time on the sleds. All too soon, it was time for her to leave, and just like old times, Diamond whinnied a loud good-bye as her taillights disappeared down the driveway.

U U

It's been a very long time since my stint up at that guest ranch, and the other day I was looking through some old pictures and found one I'd almost forgotten I had. It's a close-up photo of Diamond with his head down, eyes half-closed, standing beside Anne as she is reaching up and petting him on the neck. In the photo, Diamond's head seems as big as Anne's entire body, and the softness he is offering her is unmistakable.

I have come to understand that horses always remember those things that are important to them. If I were a betting man, I'd wager that big horse doesn't have any trouble at all remembering that little girl who just showed up at the barn one day all those years ago—the one he so kindly let stand on a bucket and clumsily toss harness over his back. The one he helped land a job ... and the one he undoubtedly considered to be his friend.

CHAPTER 8

Housetraining

"The best teachers aren't always those on two legs."

I spent most of the morning setting T-posts so I could cross-fence one of our pastures. It was about lunchtime, so I figured I might as well take a break before stringing the wire and hunt me up some lunch at the house. As I walked into the kitchen, Wendy was already there, building me a ham sandwich.

"How's the fencing going?" she asked, setting the plate down on the counter that separated the kitchen from the dining room.

"Pretty good," I told her. "I should be able to get most of the wire strung by the end of the day."

I took off my hat and coat and hung them on one of the dining room chairs.

"Thanks for the sandwich," I said, as I took my seat at the counter.

Because our schedules rarely matched up during the day, I usually had to fend for myself at lunchtime, so it was a pleasant surprise to find Wendy in the house and taking the time to make me a sandwich.

"How's your day going?" I asked, taking a bite.

"Pretty good," she said, filling a glass of water and placing it on the counter next to my plate. "I got most of the office work done."

She went back to the refrigerator and took out a plastic container that held leftover spaghetti from the night before.

"I was listening to the radio this morning," she said, opening the container and forking some of the spaghetti onto a plate. "You know they do that pet report at ten o'clock or so."

"No," I said, as I started to get a feeling about why our schedules had just happened to match up for lunch that day, "I didn't know they did a pet report."

"Well," she said, as she placed her plate in the microwave, "they do. And today they said they had this border collie-Australian shepherd mix puppy up for adoption." The microwave buttons beeped as she punched them, and the machine started heating her food. "It sounds like a real nice little dog. Evidently someone abandoned it somewhere in town, and they've had him for a couple weeks."

"I see," I said, already having a pretty good idea where this was going.

"What would you think about going down and taking a look at him?"

"I don't think that's such a good idea," I said, having paused to give the proposal a little thought. "We don't really need another dog right now."

During that short pause, all I could think of was that we already had two dogs, Sadie and Patch, both of whom were grown and knew the ropes around the place. We were just coming into the spring of the year, one of my busiest times at the ranch, and because I usually did most of the training when it came to our dogs, I didn't think I would have the time right then that a pup would require.

"I know we don't *need* one," she replied, "but it might be nice to have one."

"I just don't think so," I repeated, a little more sympathetically. "Not right now, anyway."

Wendy went quiet for a few seconds.

"You're probably right," she agreed, although I knew she didn't. "I'm sure they'll find him a good home."

"I'm sure they will."

I didn't hear anything about the pup for another two days. But on the third day I came home for supper and went into the office where Wendy was finishing her work. Without even looking up from her computer, she said, "That pup was on the pet report again today. Maybe we should go have a look at him."

"We just don't need another dog right now," I said, trying to be firm.

"I know," she said, turning around and looking at me, "but I feel like he's just sitting there calling to me."

I had to think about that for a minute. Wendy and I had been together for a long time, and in that time I'd never heard her make a statement like that. To be honest, I wasn't sure whether she was kidding or not. But one thing I did know for sure, if she wasn't kidding, the next words out of my mouth had better be very carefully chosen.

"Well," I said, after several seconds of silence, "how about this? Tomorrow is Friday. If the pup is still on the pet report tomorrow, give them a call and we'll go down and have a look at him on Saturday. But if he looks like he's going to be too much work, we're going to have to leave him."

I had no idea what I meant by the pup being "too much work." Heck, all pups are a lot of work. I guess maybe I was just grasping at straws, trying to leave myself an excuse for leaving him there … knowing full well it probably wouldn't work anyway.

Wendy did, indeed, listen to the pet report the next day, and the pup was still there. True to my word, the following day we went down and took a look at him. It was kind of interesting. When we got to the vet's office where the animals were being adopted out, the woman behind the counter began telling us about the pup.

"He's a really sweet little guy," she said, "but he does have a lot of energy. If we'd let him, he'd just play all day out back there."

"We know about working dogs," I smiled.

"Okay," she said, as if she was trying to warn us about this little Tasmanian devil she was about to bring out. "I just didn't want you to be surprised."

She went into the back room, and a few minutes later she re-appeared with this little black pup bounding in front of her on a leash. He had the white border collie cape over his shoulders and white on his legs. He was a little older than I expected, six months, and at some point in his short life, someone had docked his tail. That didn't stop him from trying to wag it, though, and as he charged into the room, his whole body wiggled furiously back and forth in glee that someone had actually come to say hello to him.

Wendy immediately knelt down, and the pup ran up and started licking her face.

"See what I mean about him having all this energy?" the woman asked, as if she were a little embarrassed by the dog's behavior.

"How much time does he get outside?" I questioned.

"About an hour or so each day," she said. "The rest of the time he's in his cage in back."

Not near enough time outside for a working dog like this, I thought. *No wonder he's bouncing off the walls.*

"Oh, he's not so bad," Wendy said with a smile. "He's just happy to see somebody."

She was right. The little guy was going stir crazy cooped up in that little cage they had him in. *Besides*, I thought, *being an older pup might make him a little easier to work with as far as training, if someone hadn't already done so.*

After hanging out with him for several minutes, it was becoming clear he was a very nice dog, and Wendy was looking to me to make a decision.

"If we were to take him," I asked, as I knelt down and began petting the little guy, "and he just doesn't work out, can we bring him back?"

"Of course," the woman smiled.

"Is he housebroke?" I asked.

"Not as far as we can tell," she replied, almost as if hoping that wouldn't be a deal breaker.

"I think he'll be okay," Wendy smiled. "How is he with kids and other dogs?"

"As far as we can tell, he's fine with both. When he's outside here he plays with all the other dogs, and we've had a couple families come look at him and he's been great with even the smallest kids."

That was all Wendy needed to hear. The next thing you know we had the little guy in the truck and were heading back to the ranch.

Later that morning, we introduced the pup, whom we decided to name Bill, to our other two dogs. Our older dog Sadie, while pleasant enough to him, acted more like she would tolerate him for now but would be just as happy if we took him back where he came from. Patch, on the other hand, thought Bill was quite possibly the cutest thing she'd ever seen and immediately took him under her wing.

For the rest of the day, wherever Patch went, so did Bill, and wherever Bill went, Patch wasn't far behind. It was almost as if Patch knew the pup needed to run off some energy and saw it as her duty to help him do so. The two of them played together nonstop for nearly four hours. And when Patch wasn't playing with Bill, one or more of the kids was. By mid-afternoon, the exuberant pup we had seen in the vet's office was more than ready for a good nap, which he took by simply flopping down under a tree in the backyard.

After Bill burned off some of that steam he had accumulated during his stay at the vet's place, his true nature began to show itself. He was indeed a very good dog that tried hard to please everyone he came in contact with, whether it was one of the other dogs, one of the kids, or Wendy and me. I suppose it was because of that willingness he showed so soon after coming to our home that we decided he would be staying with us for good.

♘ ♘

Really the only "training" we did with Bill that day was start teaching him his name. Other than that, we just sort of let him get a sense for who we were and where he was. Our dogs always spend the majority of the day outside, either on the ranch with me or in our large, enclosed backyard. They spend the night, however, in the house. By nightfall on Bill's first day with us, he was obviously pretty tired.

After dark we brought him in the house along with the other two dogs, where they mostly just hung out until it was bedtime. As we did every evening before we turned in, we let the dogs out one last time. Usually, Sadie and Patch had the run of the house after we went to bed. They were both housebroken, of course, and we knew we didn't have to worry about either one as far as "accidents" went. However, we'd already discovered the hard way during the evening that Bill wasn't housebroken, and so rather than letting him run loose with the big dogs and possibly making a mess on the carpet, we decided to put him in the kitchen where accidents would be easier to clean up.

We put Patch in the kitchen with him that night to keep him company and put up a little barricade to keep them in. Once we were confident he couldn't make an escape, we turned in for the night.

Now, I fully intended to get up during the night and let the pup outside in hopes of warding off any more accidents, but unfortunately I guess I was just tired enough to sleep through that little plan. When we got up in the morning and went to the kitchen, we were met with what can only be described as a "puppy-waste disaster area."

As we came around the corner, we found Patch sitting on what looked like the only clean spot on the floor. The expression on her face was one that clearly stated she had *not* been the one to create this mess. As we stood looking over the temporary barricade, Patch looked at the mess, then looked at the pup, and then turned and looked at us. She repeated this behavior several times, as if to say, *Surely you know* he *did this, right?* The pup, by the way, was sitting as close to the back door as he possibly could, ears flat to his head and eyes as sad as they could be, staring up at the doorknob.

We let all three dogs outside, cleaned up the mess in the kitchen, and got on with the rest of our day. That night, we put Patch and Bill together in the kitchen and again put up our makeshift barricade. The following morning we got up, fully expecting a repeat of the mess we'd found the day before, but much to our surprise both Bill and Patch met us at the little barricade, both of them with their heads up and tails wagging.

There were no messes at all in the kitchen that morning … nor have there been any morning since, from that day to this.

U U

Somehow—and without us ever having to work with him on it at all—Bill had miraculously become housebroken, and he got that way literally overnight. The only other individual with him was our dog Patch.

Now I suppose common sense tells us Bill may have already been housebroken to some extent when we got him, and all the excitement of his first day with us was just too much for the little guy. And, well, accidents do happen.

On the other hand, there is the possibility that he wasn't housebroken, and it may actually have been Patch who somehow communicated to him the finer points of being a house dog. I guess in the end we'll just never really know for sure.

I will say this, though. Since that time back when Bill was a pup, we've raised three more border collie puppies. And, by golly, if Patch did have a hand in helping Bill learn to be housebroken, I sure wish she had let us in on her secret.

CHAPTER 9

The Dun Colt

"If we don't do it now, we'll pay for it later."

Some time ago, when Wendy and I were still at the guest ranch, we got into the horse-breeding business. I suppose we hoped somewhere down the line it would turn into a going concern and make some money for us, but at the time we weren't really interested in that. Mostly it was just a way to ensure the quality of the horses we'd be getting from one year to the next, instead of buying replacement horses for the string that came from Lord knows where and toting with them who-knew-how-many training issues.

I bought some good, proven quarter horse brood mares from a friend up in Minnesota, along with an older foundation-bred quarter horse stallion from my buddy Dwight, and began raising babies that eventually turned into real nice horses.

We continued our breeding program after we left the ranch, raising a batch of two to four babies a year. We always used the same stallion and brood mares and, as a result, always got foals with good minds that were athletic, good-boned, and easy to work with.

Unfortunately, as the years passed and I began spending more and more time on the road, Wendy was left to do all the work by herself. This meant not only tending to the stallion, mares, babies, and all our other horses, but also running the household, raising three kids, working part-time at the church, and being the volunteer coordinator at the kids' school. It became clear we couldn't continue the breeding program because neither one of us had the time to devote to it.

We'd already bred three of our four mares at the time we made our decision, and we decided we wouldn't sell the mares until all the babies were on the ground, in case we ended up with one we just couldn't live without. We did sell our stallion, however, so we wouldn't be tempted to change our minds. Then we sat back and waited for our last crop of babies to arrive.

We got lucky in that all three mares foaled pretty much at the same time. The first mare, Shiloh, had a real nice sorrel filly sometime during the night on Monday. Two nights later both Medora and Ellie had their foals. Medora had a little bay colt, and Ellie had a dun colt.

The filly and the bay colt were pretty much exactly what we'd expected to get from those two mares—quiet, healthy young-sters with good minds and easy-going dispositions. That dun colt of Ellie's … now he was another story.

U U

Almost right away we could see something wasn't right with Ellie's colt. First we noticed that whenever he nursed, milk spilled from his nose. This is usually a sure sign the baby has a cleft palate, which allows the milk to enter the nasal cavity through a hole in roof of the mouth. A few weeks after the colt was born, the vet came out for a routine visit and confirmed my suspicions.

A cleft palate can be surgically corrected, but we hesitated to do so. What made us hesitate and bothered us even more was this colt's odd behavior toward people. In the past, these three mares had always thrown very gentle and good-minded babies, and the first two in this lot were certainly true to form. But the dun colt seemed far from being gentle or good-minded.

When he first saw us, he became panic stricken, and he con-tinued to do so at the sight of any human, so much so that he often ran blindly into the wall if one of us even looked into the stall he and his mother were in. If we approached him, he nearly threw himself over backwards trying to get away.

When we finally got our hands on him that first day, he put up such a fight I thought he was either going to kill himself or one of us in the process. When he finally calmed down, it was more from sheer exhaustion than any kind of understanding of what we were asking of him. As bad as this behavior was, I knew we needed to get some kind of a handle on it as quickly as possible, so he would at least be manageable for the vet or farrier … and for us, for that matter.

So, over the next several weeks I worked with him whenever I could, and I tried my darnedest to keep the anxiety level low. Unfortunately, as hard as I tried, I don't feel I was very successful. While he could be haltered (if you could get close enough to get a hand on him) and he could be led to some extent, neither one was pretty. He was still prone to panic from time to time just out of the blue, and he often crashed into things in an attempt to get away from monsters seen only by him.

His behavior baffled me for sure, but I believe Wendy summed it up best when she said to me one day, "You know, the way that colt acts is just downright scary." And she was right.

The other two babies came along just fine. They were easy to catch and halter, learned how to lead without any trouble, and were good with their feet and with getting in and out of a trailer. The vet and farrier had no trouble working with them, and they were very social with us and each other. Not the dun colt. He was flighty and unpredictable, shook uncontrollably whenever someone handled him, and was antisocial around everybody with the exception of his mom.

He never did get the hang of leading properly, so to see if I could help him with the idea, I ponied him off Ellie. I quickly found he had no trouble following her and never paid any mind to me up on her back. After working with him several times from his mom's back and then trying again to lead him from the ground or pony him from another horse, it was plain to see he still wasn't getting the idea.

I must admit, as time went on, I began thinking this was not a colt we were going to keep. In fact, due to his unpredictable and dangerous nature, I seriously considered putting him down. In talking with my vet about the colt's behavior, he suggested the cleft palate might not have been this colt's only birth defect; he may have experienced some kind of brain damage as well. Vets at a large-animal hospital told me that while brain damage like this is not common in babies, it isn't uncommon either and certainly could be (and probably was) at the heart of this issue.

Still, I really struggled with the idea of putting a physically healthy colt to sleep, and so I put off thinking about it for several weeks. I also put off working with the little guy during that time because of the stress it caused both of us. Before I knew it, a number of months had passed, and it was time for the herd to go to winter pasture.

Wendy and I decided to turn the colt out with all the other horses and see how he did. We hoped getting him away from people for a while might improve his feelings toward us, and besides, it was really the only thing we hadn't tried in our attempts to help him. However, we also decided if he didn't show any improvement by spring, we would probably put him down.

♘   ♘

So the dun colt went on pasture along with the rest of our herd of eighteen head, ranging in ages from a few months to nineteen years old. Once or twice a week Wendy and I made the thirty-five mile trip to check on them. We always made a point of getting up close to every horse to make sure they didn't have any cuts or other injuries, and very seldom did we find any. Most of the horses in our herd had been together for a number of years and had worked out the pecking order long ago. There was plenty of good grass and fresh water to go around, and things on the pasture were pretty peaceful.

Although we had hoped being on the pasture and away from people would help the colt settle down some and be more accepting of us, after two months out with the herd, we weren't seeing any improvement. If anything, the open space of the pasture only served to keep him farther away whenever we came around, even though his mother was often the first to approach when we did our "hands-on" check of the horses.

Still, I wasn't ready to throw in the towel on the dun colt just yet. Every once in a while I would make an attempt to get close to him, and sometimes I *was* able to get within a few feet, but seldom any closer. He was getting bigger now, in spite of the fact he still suffered from the cleft palate. The white crust we were used to seeing on his nose and muzzle from nursing had been replaced by a greenish-colored crust. Apparently some of the grass he was eating was being caught up in the hole in the roof of his mouth and expelled from his nostrils ... not a very attractive sight.

♘ ♘

One day along about mid-January I made a trip alone to check the horses. I pulled through the east gate and couldn't see any of them. That wasn't uncommon since the herd had the run of the full eighty acres and was often out of sight at the far west end.

As I drove along the dirt road inside the pasture, I soon came upon Ellie grazing by herself about a quarter-mile in. I thought it a little strange she was off by herself, but I continued on west.

The dirt road ran along the southern irrigation ditch, which held water all year and was the primary water source for the herd. The ditch bank was anywhere from four to nearly ten feet high, and there were only a couple of places sloped enough for the horses to get down to drink, one in the middle of the pasture and the other at the west end.

A lot of ducks wintered in the ditch, and they often flew up unexpectedly, splashing water and making a ruckus as I drove along the road. As I passed Ellie, who was 200 yards out in the pasture to my right, my attention was on her, but to the left, out of the corner of my eye, I saw what I assumed to be ducks flying out of the ditch. Water splashed for sure, but the bank there was so deep I couldn't see down in the ditch to be certain, and I didn't pay it much mind.

I continued to drive, and just past the middle point of the pasture, I found the rest of the herd grazing peacefully. I made a quick count, as I always did, and came up one head short, even including Ellie. I counted again and still came up short.

I drove to the west end of the pasture, thinking one of the horses might have been down getting water, but that wasn't the case. I returned to the herd and counted again, with the same results. By checking their colors, I discovered which horse was missing—Ellie's dun colt.

At first I wasn't too concerned, figuring he'd probably just wandered off and hid in some of the willows that grew sporadically along the ditches on both sides of the pasture. But then I remembered Ellie off by herself and that splash of water in the ditch.

I hurriedly drove east along the ditch until I was near Ellie. I stopped the truck and got out for a closer inspection of the ditch, concentrating on the area where I thought I'd seen the splash. At first I didn't see or hear anything out of the ordinary, but I continued walking the ditch. As I rounded a curve in the bank, there he was. Somehow, the dun colt had fallen into the ditch at unquestionably the worst place he could have.

The banks on both sides were the steepest of anywhere on the property. From where I was standing, the slope went down eight feet to the ditch bank, where there was a sheer, two-foot drop to the water. This drop-off made it impossible for the colt to climb out of the water. The water was also deepest here at about five feet, deep enough to cover the colt's back but not his head.

Twenty feet in either direction, the water became considerably more shallow, and the banks had a more gradual slope.

While still difficult to climb, it would at least be possible for the colt to get up them.

As it was, however, the colt was in big trouble. He had broken through the thin layer of ice covering the water in that particular spot, and it was obvious the freezing-cold water was taking a toll on him. Even so, as I watched him struggle, I had to hand it to him. As cold and weak as he was, he was still trying to find a way out.

Its funny how the mind works when faced with a situation like this. My first inclination was to go to the truck, get the gun, and put the colt out of his misery ... particularly considering we had been leaning in that direction anyway.

But then something else took over—something that tells you all of this must have happened for a reason. There was a reason he fell in the ditch right in that very spot, where it was impossible for him to get out on his own. There was a reason I came down to check horses by myself that day and a reason I found him before he either froze to death or drowned. I thought about the problem and watched the poor little guy struggle in the water for a minute before going back to the truck to get my rope.

The ditch bank was almost too steep to navigate, so from the top of the bank I built a loop and tossed it down over his head, catching him around the neck. I hoped to ease him to a shallow part of the ditch where he could get his footing and scramble up the bank. It was a good plan and more than likely would have worked with any of our other colts, but I quickly found out it wasn't going to work with this one.

Evidently, I'd made a mistake in thinking the colt was exhausted and half froze to death. As soon as I took up the slack, I sure found out different. Even though I'd moved slowly so as not to scare him too much, he began thrashing about and fighting the rope. I only had a thirty-foot rope with me at the time, and I don't mind telling you, with him carrying on like he was, I came to the end of it pretty quick.

I found myself being pulled down the steep bank toward the water. I was in a pickle for sure. One wrong move on that steep bank, and I knew I'd be in the drink. But if I let go of the rope, the colt was sure to pull it in the water, eliminating any chance I'd have to help him out of this mess.

One thing for sure, I was determined not to end up in the water with that colt. With him thrashing around like he was (and not liking people all that much to begin with), the chances of either one of us getting out alive wouldn't be good at all.

So I dug in as best I could and for the first few minutes just tried not to get pulled in. While I did that, the colt threw himself violently backwards over and over again, moving even farther out into the deepest part of the ditch. After a few minutes, he went a little limp from exhaustion or fear, and I figured that was my opportunity to try to get him closer to my side of the ditch. I slowly reeled him in, like a big fish, and he sort of floated toward me as I did.

Everything was going along just fine until his feet made contact with the shallow bottom near the bank. As soon as that happened, he again began throwing himself violently back into the middle of the ditch and the deep water. This scenario played itself out over and over again for the next forty-five minutes.

During that time, I was doing everything I could to stay up on the bank, which was so steep it made it nearly impossible just to stand, much less maneuver around or to even handle the rope efficiently. My options for helping the colt were extremely limited, and I found myself simply trying to keep his head above water so at least he wouldn't drown.

While I certainly wasn't going through the kind of physical trauma the colt was, I was in fact experiencing some of my own problems. You see, because of the steepness of the bank, I was forced to stand with my feet pointed almost straight down, sort of like a ballerina—which I am not, nor will I ever be.

Standing like this obviously jammed my toes up tight into the toes of my Ropers, and I don't mind telling you that got uncomfortable pretty darn fast. Standing like this also put tremendous stress on every joint and muscle in my entire body. You see, in an attempt to keep myself upright and balanced, my body took the shape of a backward "C." My feet were sort of behind me, which caused my knees to bend, which pushed my hips forward, which caused my back to arch so that my head ended up over my feet.

Within just a few minutes, the muscles in my shins, calves, thighs, arms, shoulders, and back all began to ache and burn like I was in some sort of workout video. And the unfortunate thing for both of us was we still had a long way to go before this situation was going to be rectified.

Well, after about forty-five minutes, the colt finally appeared to be running out of steam, which was good, because so was I. It took that long before I could move the colt to the shallow part of the ditch without him immediately flopping over backwards. He still couldn't (or wouldn't) stand up, though, and just lay there in the freezing water with his nose and mouth just barely above the surface. I was able to get him to stay in the shallow water and relax on a couple of occasions, but as soon as I put tension on the rope to urge him closer to the bank, he would once again begin thrashing around.

Another half hour passed without much progress and with sheer exhaustion beginning to set in for both of us, it was time for me to realistically weigh my options.

There was no telling how long the colt had been in the water before I got to him. One thing I did know, however, was he had been in it for going on two hours since I'd shown up. Not only that, but he'd spent at least some of that time totally submerged—head and all—and in the last fifteen minutes or so, it was getting increasingly harder for me to keep him from going under. Physically, I had pushed myself about as far as I could, and I used every quiet minute he offered to sit on my backside on the slope.

His breathing had become more labored, and the rattle coming from his nostrils on every exhale told me he more than likely had water in his lungs. I don't mind telling you this was one of those situations that just makes you sit and scratch your head. This little guy had been fighting like crazy to stay alive, but every single time he got to where he might actually be able to help himself out of his predicament, he seemed to fight just as hard to stay in it.

It was time for a decision, and as much as I hated to say it, I told myself I would try only one more time to get him to shore. If it didn't work out, for whatever reason, I would simply have to put him down. Having committed myself to this decision, I got to my feet and gave it one last try.

At first, the colt resisted just as he had every time before, thrashing his head and neck in the water and trying to flip over backward. Then, just as I was ready to throw in the towel, he suddenly stopped fighting. His resignation was fast and so complete it was almost as if someone flipped a switch. He went from flinging himself around like one of those big, deep-sea fish, to being the docile little colt we thought we would have on the day he was born.

He let me quietly bring him back to the shallow part of the ditch where we had been countless times already. Unfortunately, he was so exhausted he couldn't stand up, much less climb over the edge of the ditch to get out of the water and then scramble up the steep slope to dry ground.

I was forced to go to plan "B." This would entail somehow dragging the colt upstream another fifteen feet or so, where the water in the ditch was only inches deep and the slope of the bank was much more gradual. If I could move him there, my chances of getting him out successfully would greatly increase.

Still, my body had gone through about as much as it could take, and I had very little fuel left in the tank. The bank I had to traverse to move him over to the shallow part of the ditch was even steeper than where I'd been standing, and to make matters worse, there was a fairly large willow bush in the way. Still, it was really our only option, and I figured as long as he stayed quiet, we had a chance.

I took a deep breath, coiled the loose end of the lariat in my hands, took a good grip, and started my trek along the bank. The colt struggled a little bit, but seemed pretty resigned to being pulled along, as if he knew this was really his last chance.

Those fifteen feet were by far the greatest distance I ever traveled ... before or since. The pain in my feet, legs, back, and shoulders was bad, and at one point I remember thinking I was going to sleep real good that night. Anyway, as I slowly pulled him through the water, I somehow got the colt close enough to the bank that I had enough rope to make my way to the top of the bank. For the first time in two hours, I was able to walk on level ground. This was good, because it gave me some maneuvering room around the steepest part of the bank, as well as around the willow bush. While the rope did get hung up in the bush a couple times, I was able to get past it.

Once around the bush, the bank sloped more gradually to the water, and I eased myself down. The colt was lying on his side with his head just above the water's surface. I got to the edge of the ditch and pulled him as close as I could, about four feet from the bank, where he sort of ran aground on the rocky bottom.

The water around the colt was about two feet deep, but where I was standing it was only six inches deep. I waded in the icy water and dragged the colt as close to me as I could. He moved around some but not nearly as bad as he had for the past two hours, and I quickly moved him to within a couple feet of me. At this point I was finally able to reach down and stroke him on his neck and head. I loosened the rope around his neck to allow him to breathe better and found it helped a little but not much.

At this point, I had moved the colt as far as I could using the rope around his neck, and with him being as worn out as he was, I decided he'd probably stay put if I left him for a couple of minutes. With that, I wearily climbed the bank and went to my truck. I drove it back along the road and parked as close to the colt as I could. I took a small halter with a lead rope from the toolbox and headed back to the colt.

The colt was right where I'd left him, and he put up no resistance as I put the halter on, removed the rope from around his neck, and re-looped it around both of his front legs. Then, holding the lead rope in my right hand and the lariat looped around his front legs in my left, I slowly began dragging him to dry ground.

I was pretty well spent, and it took everything I had just to get his head, neck, and shoulders on the grass of the bank. Once I got him that far, I plopped down heavily in the grass next to his head, knowing I'd done as much as I could. As much as I wanted to get him up the bank and onto the road, I simply wasn't physically able to do it.

Coming to that realization, I removed the rope from the colt's front legs and looped it around both hind legs. I walked to the truck and tied the other end of the rope to the ball of the trailer hitch. I climbed in, and keeping a close eye on the colt and going as slowly as I could, I drove the truck forward and eased the colt out of the ditch, up the embankment, and finally onto the road.

Ellie, who had been grazing out in the pasture all this time, suddenly took notice. Her head popped up out of the grass, and with ears erect, she let out a low nicker as the colt appeared on the road. The colt didn't respond to her, and as I removed the rope from around his hind legs, I began to think this had all been for naught.

He was literally soaked to the bone, his lungs rattled unsettlingly with every breath, and he was limp and unresponsive. I took off my jacket and began to dry him off with it. Ellie made her way over to him and licked and nuzzled him as if he were a newborn.

Luckily, it was a relatively mild day for the middle of winter, and now that the colt was up on the road, he was getting the full warming effects of the midday sun. I dried him off as best I could, and then, completely exhausted, I dropped the tailgate and took a seat while deliberating on what my next move should be.

While I was thinking, Ellie went to work on reviving the waterlogged colt. After nuzzling and licking him for a little while, she began nipping him on the flank and neck. At first, her nips were pretty gentle, barely grazing the skin. But soon, her nips became much more enthusiastic. Eventually the colt began to stir and appeared to come back to life. In time, he even let out a little raspy nicker of his own, and the mare became even more vigorous in her encouragement.

The colt finally tried to lift his head several times, only to have it fall back down. Undeterred, the mare kept after him, and soon he not only raised his head and neck, but was also trying to lift himself up onto his front legs. I decided to get in and help, too. I left my relatively comfortable spot on the tailgate and went over to the colt. Each time he tried to get to his feet, I wrapped my arms around his barrel and tried to lift him. I'm not sure how much help I actually was, seeing as how I had little strength of my own, but between Ellie, the colt, and me, he eventually made it all the way to his feet.

Not long afterwards, he was nursing his mother, and he slowly regained enough strength to move a little. I slowly led the two of them down the road to the catch pen a half-mile to the west. It took a good hour for the three of us to get there. I closed the two of them in and left them there while I drove home and got a trailer.

I brought both of them back home, put them in a big stall in the barn, and called the vet. At first, the vet's prognosis wasn't good. The colt had not only swallowed a great deal of water, he had also aspirated a bunch of water as well. This would almost certainly lead to pneumonia or some other kind of infection in his lungs, the vet thought. He was eating and nursing some, but not very well, and he was extremely lethargic and dull to any kind of stimulus.

Still, the vet suggested we keep him warm and as comfortable as possible for the next couple days and give him antibiotics. Then we'd take another look and make a decision on what to do with him. If he wasn't any better, then it might be best just to put him to sleep. However, if he showed signs of improvement, we'd keep doing what we were doing and see what transpired.

Well, much to everyone's surprise, the colt slowly but surely began to make a recovery, and after about three weeks, he was pretty much back to his old self ... with one major exception. He was much easier to handle than he had been before.

Oh, don't get me wrong here. He was still a little spooky and could sometimes be hard to catch, but overall he was considerably better behaved and seemed to have a lot more try in him, as far as wanting to figure out what we were asking of him.

Two months later, with spring just around the corner, the colt had made a full recovery. He was also leading much better, allowed his feet to be handled and trimmed without incident, and didn't even mind too much seeing the vet come around.

Still, there was the issue of his cleft palate. Wendy and I had already made up our minds we weren't going to put the money into surgery for him, but figured if someone else wanted to, that was fine with us.

Interestingly enough, not long afterwards, an older retired rancher contacted us looking for a young horse he could just sort of play with and raise up. This fellow didn't have any big aspirations for the colt but was willing to spend the money on surgery for him and just sort of take his time with the training.

It seemed like a perfect fit, and soon the colt was on a trailer heading for his new home on a ranch out on the plains of Colorado.

It's funny... we raised an awful lot of good colts over the years, some of which we still have to this day. Yet, the one that's the most memorable for me is that little dun colt with the cleft palate. I often think about how, had he and I not had our adventure in the ditch that day, I might have very easily dismissed him and perhaps even put him down. I might have never seen the good in the little colt, the fight in him, and the fire to stay alive ... even though, admittedly, his life wasn't one I initially found much worth in. The memory of him has given me pause on more than one occasion for that very reason.

Whenever I think about that dun colt, I wonder how he did with that old rancher and whatever became of the two of them. Even more than that, however, I wonder what *my* life would have been like had he never come along at all.

CHAPTER 10

Team Penning with Dwight and Dave

"Be quick but don't hurry."

Dwight had about thirty cow/calf pairs he needed to move to better grass, so we went out early one Sunday morning to get it done. We found most of the herd spread out among the trees on the far western edge of the big pasture, but it didn't take long to bunch them up in a small clearing and sort the pairs he needed.

We spent the rest of the morning slowly moving them a mile or so to the east, across a large wooden bridge and through the gate that opened up to the forty-five acres of grass where they would spend the next month or so. It was warm for early October, and our horses were already haired up pretty good for the winter. As a result, by the time we finished moving the herd to the pasture and closed the gate behind them, the horses had worked up a bit of a sweat. Even so, we rode back up to the barn, pulled the bridles off our ponies, loosened their cinches, and loaded them into the back of Dwight's stock trailer.

The night before, I had gotten a call from a friend of ours, Dave Schneider, who asked if we wanted to go down to Ft. Collins that day and ride in a jackpot team-penning competition. Neither Dwight nor I had ever done any team penning (in fact, at the time we really didn't even know what it was), so more out of curiosity than anything else we agreed to give it a try.

An hour or so later, we met Dave at the team-penning competition. He pulled his horse, a quarter horse gelding named Little John Beam or John, for short, out of his beat-up, old two-horse trailer, and Dwight and I jumped our geldings, both complete with dried sweat and saddles still strapped to their backs, out of the stock trailer.

I must say, we definitely stuck out among the slick-haired, high-dollar horses that were being pulled out of the expensive trailers that surrounded us, and to be honest, it didn't take very long for us to feel just a little out of place. Even so, we tied our horses to the trailer and made our way over to the sign-up table to pay our entry fee.

At the time, team penning was a relatively new event, new enough that none of us had heard much about it, other than you needed three riders to make up a team and each team needed to do something with cattle. So while we were waiting there in line, we decided to ask some of the other participants what the rules were. One young fellow with a $400 beaver hat and a belt buckle as big as his head explained how it was done.

In the nearby arena, there were thirty head of medium-sized roping steers. The steers had been split into ten groups of three steers each, and each group had a number. Each steer was wearing the number of its group on its hip. So, three steers were wearing number 1, three were wearing number 2, and so on. The thirty steers then milled around in the arena.

Each team of riders would draw a number out of a hat corresponding to a group of steers. The team would ride into the arena together, sort the three steers out of the herd, take them down to the other end of the arena, and put them in a three-sided pen. Team penning is a timed event, and once the three steers were in the pen, you raised your hand to stop the clock.

"So," Dwight said, almost not believing what he had just heard, "you need three riders to sort and move three steers?"

"Yeah," the kid said. "It can get pretty exciting."

"I bet," Dwight nodded slightly.

The young guy moved up to the registration table with the rest of his team.

"Seems like it'd be more sporting if you only used one rider for three steers," Dwight said quietly, turning to Dave and me. "But it's their game, so I guess we go by their rules."

A few minutes later we signed up, paid our money, and drew our number for the first go-round. As luck would have it, we drew the group of steers with number 1 on their hips, and so we would be the first team to have a go.

While we waited for the competition to start, a number of riders and even spectators came up to us and gave us pointers on the best way to cut our steers out and move them into the three-sided pen.

"Obviously," one rider, who looked more like he belonged in an office than on a horse, told us, "the faster you ride, the quicker your time."

"Thanks for the advice," I remember saying, knowing full well that trying to move cattle in a hurry is usually a recipe for disaster.

It seemed most folks felt kind of sorry for us ... as if three guys on hairy horses would never stand a chance against the other well-seasoned teams on expensive horses. To be honest, we didn't know if we stood a chance either, but one thing we did know for sure—and so did our horses—was how to work cattle, so at least we had that going for us. We figured as long as we didn't make fools of ourselves, at least we'd have a little fun. And besides, if nothing else, there was a nice barbecue lunch included in the registration fee.

As we rode our ranch horses to the arena, we could hear subtle snickers from some of the other riders as we passed by. I suppose we seemed a little out of place, and by the looks of some of those other athletic horses, a little out of our league. But we decided to have a go anyway.

We rode in and, without saying a word to each other, just went about our business. Dwight rode forward and eased his big red horse in among the herd. He found the first steer with a number 1 on its hip and eased him out along the rail. I rode my horse, Buck, over to the little steer, and at a good fifteen feet away, parked myself between him and the herd. A few seconds later, Dwight eased the second number 1 steer out, and Dave moved him up beside the steer I was holding. We no sooner had those two together than Dwight rode out with the third number 1 steer.

We put the three together and slipped them down to the other end of the arena and into the three-sided pen. Dave put his hand up and our time stopped.

"Twenty-seven seconds," the voice of an older woman cracked over the cheap P.A. system. "Good job boys. That'll be a tough time to beat."

Dwight looked at Dave and me and shrugged, none of us knowing if it would be or not. We turned our steers back in with the herd and rode out of the pen. Three other riders on big, stout quarter horses rode in. We acknowledged them by nodding our heads. As they rode past us, they smirked in our direction.

"Beginner's luck, boys?" one of them asked in a slightly conde-scending way.

"Probably," Dwight said, trying to sound sincere.

We rode over and pulled our horses into a line where the other riders were waiting their turn at the cattle. We had just pulled to a stop and turned our attention to the riders in the pen when all hell broke loose in there. With two of the riders stay-ing back a ways, the third had ridden for all he was worth right into the middle of all those steers. He spilled them in just about every direction you could think of, while the other two riders turned back the steers that came their way.

The fellow who spilled the herd ran his horse back and forth along the fence line and somehow got one of the steers he was after separated and, after several failed attempts, finally moved him away from the herd and over to his partners. He turned back and, with the same kind of enthusiasm, went after another of his designated steers. Several more seconds ticked by before he got the second one sorted and over to his teammates, and it was even longer before the third was sorted.

Once the steers were gathered, all three riders whooped and hollered them to the other end of the arena and, after several failed attempts, got them into the three-sided pen.

"Fifty-eight seconds," the woman's voice said over the loud-speaker.

For the next half-hour, we watched as one team after another used pretty much the same technique to sort and pen their cattle. Needless to say, we were a little surprised at the choice of methods these boys used, but it seemed to work to our advantage as we ended up winning the go-round with our twenty-seven-second run.

We were the fourth team up during the second go-round, and things seemed to work out for us pretty much as they had in the first one. After watching the three teams ahead of us run steers from one end of the pen to the other, we eased our way in. This time I was closest to the herd when we went in so I did the sorting.

By this time, the cattle were getting a little jumpy and they moved around some when I quietly rode in on them. As luck would have it, two of our steers had paired up and were right there on the outside of the bunch. All it took to move them away from the herd was riding past them at a distance of about ten feet and tipping Buck's nose in their direction.

Both steers just took themselves away from the herd and almost stumbled over Dave and Dwight on their way out. The third steer was on the other side of the herd, but he, too, was on the outside of the bunch. I eased up and, with the slightest movement from Buck, popped him out and over to where the other two were wait-ing. We moved them down to the other end of the arena and, with minimal effort, encouraged them into the three-sided pen.

"Wow," the lady's voice said over the P.A. "Twenty-two seconds! I believe that's a new arena record!"

As the announcer's voice trailed off, a spattering of applause broke out—along with an equal spattering of groans from some of the other teams.

We knew our run was fast (we also knew it was due in large part to the lucky positioning of the steers that made gathering them incredibly easy), but we had no idea we had been *that* fast.

Our third go-round, while still pretty fast, wasn't as good as the other two. This time, Dave sorted the steers easily, but as we began to move them down the rail to the other end of the arena, some of the steers from the herd began to follow. One of the rules of team penning is that only the three steers you draw can be at the end of the arena with the three-sided pen when you move your steers into it, so one of us had to break off and move the stragglers back. I decided to do that.

I pulled Buck off our three steers to urge the stragglers back to the herd. When I did, I ever-so-briefly left a small opening between Dave and Dwight, which one of our steers spotted and took advantage of. In a flash, the little brown-and-white squirted through the opening and trotted back to the big herd, holding his head and tail high in the air as he did.

Now, when something like this had happened to some of the other teams, the spectators were quiet, with the exception of an occasional sympathetic groan. But when our steer cut back, a raucous round of applause went up from just about everyone there, as if they were actually cheering for the steer, which I guess they were.

I was able to ease into the bunch and cut the renegade steer back out without too much trouble, but by the time we got our three steers in the pen, we had lost enough time to take only second place in the go-round. When that was announced, a pretty big cheer went up again from the other teams.

The fourth and final go-round went smoothly for us, the way the first two had. We went in easy, quietly cut our steers out, and eased them down into the pen for another time well under thirty seconds. The next closest time to ours was a good fifteen seconds slower, so we had somehow won the go-round once more.

Shortly after all the teams finished that final go-round, we were summoned to the announcer's stand and awarded the prize money for the three go-rounds we had won, and for the one we placed second in. Even before we collected our money, it was painfully obvious we'd become pretty unpopular with the regulars who were there that day. Guys who had been more than willing to talk with us before the event had begun avoiding us as the day went on. Now, as we went to pick up our money, the people we passed either glared hatefully at us or ignored our presence altogether.

At first, we weren't sure why folks were so upset with us. Then as we tied our horses to the trailer and began pulling their saddles off for the trip home, a couple of riders approached who would clear things up.

"You know," one of the men said, as if he were scolding us, "this group here … none of us are professional penners. It isn't fair to come in here and sandbag us like you did, and we don't appreciate it."

Dwight and I looked at each other as Dave came over to see what was going on.

"We didn't sandbag anybody," Dwight said, matter-of-factly. "In fact, this is the first time we've ever even tried this."

"Don't give us that," the second man said. "Nobody gets the kind of times you guys did without being pro."

"Well," I piped up, "we're not. Honestly, this our first …"

Right about then, a lady rode up on a big chestnut gelding and pulled to a stop near Dave.

"You all went off without getting all your prize money," she said, reaching into a small pouch hung over her shoulder, pulling out a small wad of cash, and handing it to Dave. "Turns out you all won best go-round." She reached back in the pouch and pulled out three blue ribbons and another wad of cash, also giving it to Dave. "And you won the all-around, too."

She smiled down on a now somewhat bewildered-looking Dave, then wheeled her horse around, and rode off.

The three of us sheepishly turned to the two men standing before us.

"First time ..." the second man chuckled sarcastically. "Listen boys, a word to the wise. Next time you decide to go hustling, you should maybe think about picking a different arena. We're on to you here."

The two men turned and made their way back toward the arena.

A little stunned over this exchange, the three of us finished loading our horses and split the rest of the prize money. Each of us took one of the ribbons. We visited for a few minutes about this and that, shook hands, said our good-byes, climbed in our trucks, and headed for home.

We took the man's advice and never returned to that or any other arena to try our hand at team penning again.

♘   ♘

The money I won that day with Dwight, Dave, and our ranch horses has long ago been spent. As for the blue ribbon, well, I kept it for a while, but like the money, it too just sort of disappeared.

Yet there is one thing about that day that has definitely stayed with me over the years ... that is, even though there are those who might not appreciate a job well done, that doesn't mean the job doesn't deserve to be done well.

CHAPTER 11

Cactus Fencing

"When a proud man asks for help, it usually hurts more than you'll ever know."

Anybody who has ever spent any time on a ranch knows that keeping good fences is just one of those jobs that is never really finished. About the time you get one section in good shape, it's time to start working on another. Even if you are somehow lucky enough to get all your fences in good shape at the same time, you can rest assured it won't last … and that's just the way it is.

There are factors that can either help or hinder the overall quality of a fellow's fences, like the kind of stock he's trying to keep in or out and certainly the materials he uses to build the fence. Some folks use the best materials they can find, and obviously their fences are going to hold up better. Others … well, others use whatever they have on hand to build their fences, and those fences often need considerably more care and maintenance.

My buddy Wil was one of those guys who, more often than not, fenced using whatever he happened to have on hand. As a result, it wasn't uncommon for his fences to fall into disrepair. Wil's main pasture, on which he wintered about 130 head of saddle horses, was a 2,000-acre rectangular piece of ground in the foothills. The front part of the pasture by the road was relatively flat, but it quickly shot up about 1,000 feet in elevation.

The far north end of the pasture was fenced and had a gate that opened into an additional 500 acres up in the hills. He usually kept the gate closed until early spring. By doing this he always had that 500 to fall back on in case the winter was hard on the big pasture. He could turn the herd out on that smaller pasture until the grass started coming back along about April.

Of course, before he could turn his herd onto the 500, he would need to go around and make sure the fence that surrounded it was still standing, which is what we were doing on that unusually warm day late in March.

♆   ♆

Usually Wil enjoyed working on his fences by himself and seldom asked for help. As it turned out, he'd been fixing fence in the big pasture nearly every day for the better part of two weeks because a herd of elk kept zigzagging back and forth over his westernmost fence line. Each time the herd crossed the fence, they took the top one or two strands of wire with them. Eventually the herd moved on to terrorize someone else's fence line, but by the time they did, Wil was pretty tired of fixing fence.

I happened to run into Wil at the hardware store just about the time all the fun had gone out of fencing for him. He mentioned he could maybe use a little help checking the fence on that 500 of his the next day, if I wasn't doing anything else too pressing. As it turned out, I had the next afternoon free, so I decided to go along and give him a hand.

My truck was in the shop, so Wil picked me up, and we drove the forty minutes or so to the pasture where we saddled a couple of good horses, packed the necessary fencing tools in our saddle bags, along with a pair of binoculars for each of us, and started our ride up into the hills. About an hour later we reached the dilapidated old wire gate that opened to the 500. Wil stepped down from his horse and wrestled with the gate for a few seconds before getting it loose from its post. I held his horse while he swung it open, and I rode through leading his horse, with him closing the old gate behind us.

This 500-acre parcel was square, more or less, and covered some inhospitable country, at least along the southern fence line.

It had some very steep, rocky ravines dotted with pine trees. Mountain mahogany bushes were so thick in some places it was nearly impossible to get through them. Once you got out away from the fence line, however, there was some pretty good grass and water, and that was where the herd spent most of their time.

On this day, the plan was for me to ride east along that southern fence line and work the fence line in a counterclockwise direction. Wil would head in the opposite direction. In this way we would cover the entire fence line, checking and fixing fence along the way and meeting somewhere in the middle, all in half the time it would take Wil to do it by himself.

Obviously, the best way to check a fence is to ride right beside it. Unfortunately, the terrain along that southern line made that nearly impossible. All a fella could do in that stretch was get as close as he could, which was sometimes no more than a couple of hundred yards, inspect it as carefully as possible with the binoculars, and hope like crazy there weren't any problems to fix.

Well, I guess the terrain in that area was even a little more than the elk and deer were willing to put up with, because lucky for me, that southern line looked pretty good. Other than one little spot where a tree limb had blown down on it, the fence was tight and intact all the way to the corner.

Working north along that eastern line, however, was a different story. Almost the entire eastern fence was in open country, and it had been knocked down or loosened in a number of places. So, I spent the next two hours repairing holes and tightening loose wire all along that stretch. Eventually, I made it all the way to the northeast corner, where the last thing left to do on the eastern fence was stretch the top two wires and secure them to the corner post.

The problem I was facing was the wire all along that eastern line was very old and rusty and, therefore, brittle. Anytime I repaired a hole in the fence up to that point, I'd just cut the old rusty wire out and replaced it with some relatively newer wire I'd found hanging in bundles on some of the posts.

Leaving spare wire hanging on remote fence lines is a common practice on most ranches. That way, when you check fences, all you need to carry are your fencing tools (a fencing pliers or two, some fencing staples, a hammer). It just makes it easier to do repairs "on the fly," as it were, and saves you from having to pack a spool of wire every time you ride fence.

At any rate, I was seriously contemplating just replacing those top two wires in the corner before stretching them. About that time, Wil rode up from the west, having finished all the repairs on his half of the pasture.

"I got everything finished up to here," he said, taking his hat off and wiping the sweat from his brow with the back of his gloved hand.

"Me, too," I nodded, looking back at the corner. "I'm just debating whether or not I should replace this wire. It's about half rotted."

"Ah, hell," he said, putting his hat back on his head and climbing down from his horse. "Let's just stretch it and be done. We'll be another half-hour up here if we go to replace it."

"Sounds good to me," I shrugged. It wasn't how I would have done it, but it wasn't my fence.

Tightening a wire fence isn't all that hard, if you know how to do it. Basically you loosen the fencing staples that hold the wire to the wooden corner or anchor post it's attached to. Then, using the "pliers" part of your fencing pliers, you take hold of the wire and place the head of the pliers on the side of the post. Using the handles of the pliers for leverage, you pull the wire tight. Once you have the wire as tight as you want it, you pound the staple back in place with your hammer, securing the wire. One person can tighten or stretch wire pretty easily. But like most things, if two people are doing the job, it usually goes a little quicker.

To stretch the wire on this particular corner post, I loosened the staples holding it to the post. Wil climbed through and stood on the outside of the fence. He pulled the first wire tight with his pliers, and I pounded the staples back in place. We rewrapped the excess wire around the post. Then I loosened the staples for the second strand of wire.

Wil took hold of that wire and began to pull, just as he had with the first wire. This wire, however, didn't move as easily as the first one, so Wil put a little more muscle behind his pull. Still the wire didn't move much. Needing more leverage, Wil placed his left foot on the post and pushed. The wire slowly began to stretch into place, and once it was where we wanted it, I took my hammer and with one short swing, gave the staple a whack.

Well, with that wire being as old and rotten as it was, I guess what happened next should come as no surprise. As soon as that staple made contact with that old, rusty wire, there was a loud SNAP, and Wil suddenly went flying backwards. Evidently, the staple pinching the wire to the post was all it took to sever the crusty old thing, and I believe it was very soon after the break that Wil was wishing we'd taken the time to replace the wire.

Instinctively he let go of his pliers as he stumbled backwards several steps. He struggled to stay on his feet, but in the end, momentum and gravity took over, and he crashed backside-first into the grass. The fall didn't look all that bad, so you can imagine my surprise when he suddenly let out a blood-curdling scream, rolled to his left, and quickly pushed himself to his feet with both hands.

"You okay?" I asked, sliding through the fence to see if he was hurt.

Wil was standing stock-still with his back to me, letting out a stream of cuss words that'd make a sailor blush.

"You okay?" I repeated.

"Damn," he said as he slowly turned the palms of his gloved hands upward and looked at them. "Aaahhhhgggg."

Wil looked over his shoulder at the ground from which he had just catapulted himself and then turned his eyes toward the sky as if in disbelief.

"Cactus," was all he said, but the anguish in his voice was plain.

I looked down at the ground where he'd landed. Sure enough, he had ended up smack in the middle of a patch of little round cactus plants, the kind that grow in the foothills and mountains of Colorado. Now as far as cactus goes, this particular species isn't very big, only a couple of inches in diameter and a few inches tall. Nonetheless, it *is* still a cactus.

And in this case it wasn't just one cactus he landed on, but a whole lot of them. So many, in fact, that his entire backside was covered in cactus spines, as well as the backs of both thighs and the palms of both hands. To make matters worse, the stickers of this cactus are so strong that on more than one occasion I had felt them come through the toe of my boot.

Well, this was a problem. With all the cactus spines in his backside, Wil couldn't move, and he couldn't get the spines out of his backside because he also had spines in his hands that had gone right through his leather gloves! At first he tried to get the stickers in his hands out by himself, but trying to move his fingers was just too painful.

I offered to pull some of the spines out of his hands so he could at least get his gloves off, and he agreed. Most of the stickers were pretty big and not only easy to see but also easy to remove, and after about fifteen minutes, I had the vast majority of them out. He was then able to get his gloves off and start picking the smaller stickers from his hands by himself.

While he did that, I went back to the fence and replaced the old wire with some of the newer spare wire. About the time I finished up with that, Wil was working on trying to get some of the stickers out of his backside. He had evidently been able to pull out a number of the larger ones sticking in his jeans on his own, but getting the smaller ones was proving to be a challenge.

By this time it was mid-afternoon, and time for us to start heading back. The problem was with all the spines still in Wil's behind, he was barely able to walk, much less sit a horse. Still, he did try to cowboy up.

"I think I got enough of 'em out to where I might can walk back okay," he grunted as he struggled to put one foot in front of the other.

"You sure?" I asked, not at all convinced.

"Yeah," he groaned.

Of course, before he could even consider walking back, he first had to crawl back through the fence. I sat mesmerized as he shuffled his way over to the fence. Bending at the waist, he painfully forced himself through the fence wires that I held apart for him—it was the least I could do. He then shuffled over to his horse, picked up the reins, and agonizingly started walking for home.

I have to say, I was pretty impressed that he got as far afoot as he did, which wasn't more than about a hundred yards, and I wasn't all that surprised when he told me he couldn't go any farther. It was clear those stickers in his backside were torturing him to no end, and he would have to do something about it before we could move on.

"Man, I gotta stop," he proclaimed painfully. "I just gotta get some more of these out before they kill me."

"Fine with me," I nodded.

"I'm gonna need to drop my pants," he said.

"Go ahead," I told him. "I'm gonna go on back and make sure we got all our tools."

Now we both knew I had picked up all the fencing tools earlier, but I'm as sure as I can be there'd be nothing worse than having someone standing there looking at you while you're trying to pull cactus stickers out of your own uncovered backside. Not only that, but Wil's uncovered backside wasn't really all that high on the list of things I wanted to see that day anyway.

So, I went back to the corner where we had finished the fencing for the day and stumbled around for a while acting like I really *was* looking for misplaced tools. When I had wasted about as much time as I could, I slowly made my way back to Wil.

Wil was standing there looking pathetic, holding his pants up with one hand and his horse with the other. His face was flushed with pain, and beads of sweat stood out on his face and forehead.

"I can't get these damn things out." He was hurting for sure. "Much as I hate to say it, I'm gonna need some help."

There was an uncomfortable pause, as if neither of us was sure he'd said what he just said.

"What kind of help?" I asked hesitantly.

"Getting these damn stickers out of my ..."

"Hold on," I interrupted. "Are you sure you can't do it yourself?"

"If I thought I could do it myself, I wouldn't be asking for help!"

He had a point, and I knew he was right. Wil wasn't one to ask for help unless he really needed it. It's just that ... boy, I was sure having a hard time picturing myself doing what most certainly needed to be done.

"I wouldn't even ask," he said, shaking his head in disbelief, "but I can't feel nothing with my hands, and every time I try to get one of those stickers out, I end up pushing it in farther."

His hands *were* swollen from being full of spines earlier, and like I said, he looked pretty pathetic standing there holding his pants up. He certainly couldn't walk or ride in the condition he was in, and as much as I felt like leaving him up there to think about the kind of materials he used in his fences, in the end I guess I felt sorry for him and agreed to help him out.

"All right," I said grudgingly.

I walked closer to him, and almost in unison, we both scanned the entire wilderness area around us—and beyond—to make absolutely sure nobody was watching.

With as much dignity as Wil could muster, he painfully turned around and slowly dropped his pants to his knees. With as much dignity as I could muster, I took a deep breath, knelt down, and methodically began removing cactus spines from his behind.

After a while I had removed as many stickers as I could, and even though there were still a few more that needed to come out, they were in places only someone who has gone to medical school should be looking. Besides, now he could at least walk without being in too much pain, and if we were lucky, he could maybe even ride.

A few minutes later, we were on our way home. He was walking much better, and after going about a half-mile afoot, he decided to try to ride the rest of the way. He managed this pretty well by slowly swinging up into the saddle and standing in his stirrups as we rode back down the hill and into the yard of the ranch.

Wil fidgeted a little in his truck seat as he drove me back to town, and other than commenting about how funny a story this might be in a few years, neither one of us talked much about the incident the rest of the way. We headed into town and, almost as an afterthought, swung into the Wheel Bar for a couple of beers. When we walked in, Dwight, Bob, Delbert, and a few other ranchers and townsfolk were there. I pulled up a stool and ordered Wil and myself each a beer. Gingerly, Wil also pulled up a stool and sat down.

It was painfully obvious Will was having a hard time sitting still, and the first one to say something was Dwight.

"A little fidgety, aren't ya, Wil?" Dwight said, nonchalantly.

"Yeah." Wil glanced over at me. "I come down with a raging case of the hemorrhoids today."

"Man, I hate that," Delbert said, sounding truly sympathetic. "Most painful thing a man can go through, 'specially when you need to be all day in the saddle."

"Tell me about it," Wil said, taking a sip from his beer.

For a minute or two in that bar, I had a nearly overwhelming urge to tease Wil about ending up with a backside full of cactus spines and how funny he looked when he was trying to walk. But then, just before I actually said something, the picture of me pulling those stickers out of his behind popped into my head, and suddenly that urge subsided. After all, I guess it'd be hard to say which one would be funnier to a group of cowboys—hearing a fella explain how he got a behind full of cactus stickers, or hearing another fella explain how he ended up having to pull those stickers out of that behind.

On that particular day at the Wheel Bar, I believe it was in the best interest of both of us to simply stick with the hemorrhoid story. After all, that is one thing that never needs explaining to a group of cowboys.

CHAPTER **12**

Ghost Stories

"What you can't duck, welcome."

I don't believe in ghosts ... never did. Yet, there are some things in life that no matter how hard you try to explain them, you just can't. One such thing happened to me several years ago the night before we were to drive our herd of horses from winter pasture to the ranch, some thirty-five miles away.

Every year during the second-to-last week in March, we gathered our herd of forty-five to seventy-five horses, depending on the year, and put them on the small pasture. We'd bring in the farrier and get them shod, de-worm them, and give them their shots. By the time the first week in April came around, all the horses, with the exception of the very young and the very old, were ready for the day-long drive up to the ranch.

The night before each year's drive, I threw a small party for the hands who would be riding on the drive, with hamburgers and hot dogs, some beans and potato salad, and beer or soft drinks. The barbecue usually finished by 10:00 or 11:00 P.M. and everyone hit their bedrolls.

We usually camped under the roof of the two-sided hay barn adjacent to the pasture, rather than sleeping in tents, vehicles, or just out under the stars. The nights are still pretty cold at that time of year in Colorado, and having the roof over us kept the frost off, while the loose hay on the floor gave some extra insulation against the cold.

This year's barbecue had gone off nicely. It was good to see all the hands—including some folks I only saw once a year—there to help with the drive. By 10:30 everybody had eaten their fill, most of the stories had been told and retold, and it was time to get to bed.

The drive would start the next day before the sun was up and wouldn't finish until the sun was almost down. The hands were all experienced and knew how to tend to themselves when it came to partying the night before a full day of work. I never had to do much policing of the help before the drive ... and this night was no exception.

I was always the last one to bed and the first one up the next morning, so it was imperative I slept as well as I could. I nodded off around 11:15, and as usual, I slept pretty light. Around 2:30, two-and-a-half hours before I was to roust everybody from their bedrolls, I heard something in the dark recesses of my mind that sounded like voices.

At first they were unintelligible, and I was sure as I could be that I was dreaming. But the voices slowly grew louder, and I was able to make out a few words here and there. A short time later I opened my eyes and looked in the direction of the voices. They were coming from south of the barn, toward the pasture ... and they seemed to be heading my way.

I lay there quietly, trying to figure out by the sound of the voices which of the people from our crew had wandered out into the pasture so late in the night. But as the voices got closer, I realized I didn't recognize either one of them. Whoever was heading my way didn't belong there.

The closer the voices got, the more distinct the conversation became, and I must say, it was a very strange conversation indeed. I decided to close my eyes and act as though I was asleep in hopes of not drawing attention to the fact there was a whole crew of people in the barn they were heading for.

"Probably another couple days," the first voice said. "If'n the weather holds."

"Been a while since I seen Cheyenne," the other voice answered. "Heard it's growing up into a city."

"Me, too," came the first voice.

"Reckon we'll catch up with the wagon today?"

"About noon, I expect."

Now the voices sounded as if they were right outside the barn, not more than thirty feet from where I was lying.

"What'cha think of them two grays?" the first voice asked.

"Nice horses. Good bone on the smaller one," came the reply, as the voices entered the barn and seemed to pass within ten feet of me. Still, I kept my eyes closed and acted as if I couldn't hear them.

"Gonna need to keep an eye on them grays tomorrow," the first voice warned as the two men apparently stopped nearby. "I'd keep a rope on both of 'em, lessin they get away from ya."

"I'd say so," the second voice concurred.

The voices fell silent for a few seconds.

"Yep." It was the first voice again. "Mind them grays."

They were on the move again, heading north toward the wall of the barn.

"So, when you think we'll get there?" the second voice asked.

"Probably another couple days," was the answer. Just then the two voices apparently went right through the barn wall.

"Reckon this weather'll hold?" The voices were starting to trail off in the distance.

"Hope so, my slicker's in the wagon." Both voices chuckled as they again became indistinguishable and then faded out completely.

The night was once again silent, with the exception of an occasional snore from one of the crew, and I lay still for a few more seconds, making sure the voices hadn't doubled back. I touched the button on my watch to illuminate the face. It was 2:40 A.M., and I was definitely wide awake.

U U

A couple hours later, I roused everybody from their sleep and got the day started. After a quick breakfast, we went out and jingled in the horses we were going to use for the day. As we were grooming and tacking the horses, I nonchalantly asked around if anybody had heard anything out of the ordinary during the night. To a man, the answer was "no."

The more I thought about it, the more I started to figure the voices I'd heard must have been a dream that I had awakened from at the last minute. We continued to get ready for the day, and I pushed the whole thing out of my mind and focused my attention on the details of the drive.

To start the drive, two or three of us bunched the herd up while three others left the pasture and rode up the gravel road we had to take to get to the main road. One of these outside riders blocked a small access road just outside the gate, another rider blocked the one and only driveway a little farther down the gravel road, and the third got on the main road and was in charge of turning the herd in the direction we needed them to go.

Once everybody was in place, one of the hands opened the gate, and we eased the herd out on the road. Now the plan was always to go out at a walk and stay at a walk, if at all possible, but it never seemed to work out that way. The bottom line was, once that gate was open, you'd better be ready to ride.

This year was no exception. We'd done a nice job of gathering the herd and easing them to the gate, but once they made that turn onto the road, all hell broke loose, and we were off to the races. Luckily we were able to get the herd turned exactly where and when we needed to, and although the first two miles were done at nearly an all-out gallop, by the time we reached the first and only town we had to pass through, five miles later, the whole herd had settled nicely.

Now I say the whole herd had settled, and for the most part, they had. However, we had a pair of new horses with us this year, and they proved to be a little problematic. While the rest of the herd was trying to settle, the two new horses seemed to be doing everything they could to get them stirred up again. When that didn't work, they'd suddenly take off in some odd direction, and one or more of the hands would have to go after them and turn them back.

This continued pretty much nonstop for the first two hours of the drive, and we were all getting tired of it. I had intentionally left the new horses loose, even after they began acting up, in hopes they would eventually settle in. But they just never did.

"Mike," I called to one of the crew.

Mike was on a good sorrel gelding named Colorado, and as soon as I called to him, he was on his way over.

"You want us to get ropes on them two?" he asked, before he even got up to me.

"Yeah," I replied. "There's a couple halters and lead ropes in the trailer."

"You got it," he said, turning his horse and loping off toward the trailer we had following the herd.

I suppose it was just coincidence, but both these horses were grays. The thing that made it just a little spooky was the way Mike asked his question—the words he used were almost the same words the voices had used the night before. Those dang voices appeared to have been accurate in their warnings.

"Gonna need to keep an eye on them grays tomorrow," the first voice had warned. *"I'd keep a rope on both of 'em, lessin they get away from ya."*

It seemed the voices knew exactly what they were talking about ... more so than me, that's for sure. Those grays were new to us, but they'd been real quiet and easy to get along with up to that point. I had no reason to worry about them, unless I chose to believe the voices in the night.

Well, we got halters and ropes on the two grays. After that, the drive went without a hitch.

Still ... I do wonder about those voices from time to time.

There'd been rumors about the ghost of a playful little girl at the guest ranch for years and years. Apparently, the daughter of one of the former owners was killed in a tragic car wreck just down the road from the lodge, and right away after the accident, guests and employees alike began reporting sightings of her around the property.

Now I will be the first to say I never saw this apparition. However, I was around when some very strange things occurred. One morning I stopped by the front desk to pick up some paperwork. While I was talking with Mary, the front-desk supervisor, a young maintenance worker named Jim walked up.

"Okay," he said, placing a finished work order on the desk. "The towel rack in 102 is back up."

"Good," Mary smiled. "Now there's one down in 213." She handed him another work order and off he went.

"Man, that's weird," he said, shaking his head as he walked away.

"What's weird about that?" I asked Mary.

"He's been putting up towel racks all morning," she said, shaking her head as if in disbelief. "He gets one up in one room, and then one is down in one of the cabins. Then he gets that one up, and another one is down in the lodge. He's probably put ten up already today, and he only came on an hour ago."

"That's weird, all right," I said, picking up my paperwork and heading to the barn.

Later that day I ran into Jim at lunch and asked him about the towel racks. He told me he'd had to put nearly every towel rack in every room on the entire property back on the walls. Then, just before lunch, he got a call that the first rack he put back up when he arrived that morning was down again.

For the rest of that day, Jim did nothing but replace towel racks that had somehow become detached from walls in rooms and cabins all over the property. In the middle of the day, at the height of the problem, it seemed as though three, four, even five racks were coming loose at a time, making it impossible for him to keep up. Then, at exactly five o'clock, when it was time for Jim to leave for the day, the racks stopped coming off the walls, and the problem never occurred again.

At first, most of the employees, myself included, just assumed someone was playing a practical joke on Jim. But as time went on, it became clear from conversations between staff that that wasn't the case.

There's another thing that was kind of interesting about that day. As Jim was driving out of the driveway after his shift, he said he could have sworn he saw a little girl standing next to a tree at the front of the property, smiling and waving at him as he drove past. When he looked in his rearview mirror, she was gone.

Whether all of this was just some elaborate hoax or practical joke on Jim remains unknown. I will say this, though—if it was a joke or something like that, it sure was a good one.

♘ ♘

Not long ago I went with my assistant, Kathleen, and friends Dave Siemans and Nancy Richards to England to work some horses. While there we stayed in a little town called Okehampton. One night we all went out for a walk and came across this little tack store. The folks inside saw us peeking in the windows, and even though they were getting ready to close for the night, they invited us in to have a look around.

We all headed in different directions, looking at the various horse paraphernalia that interested us. Before long I made my way to the back of the store and came upon a small display of books beside a window. I had stopped to look at the titles when, next to me, a small plastic placard holder suddenly flew from its spot on the windowsill, nearly hitting my leg, and crashed to the floor.

Surprised, I reached down to pick it up and put it back.

"Oh, don't worry about that," the woman behind the counter said with a smile. "It happens all the time."

Not where I come from, I thought.

A little later, we were all standing up near the front of the store, visiting with the sales clerks about this and that. Suddenly, the placard holder I'd put back on the windowsill in the back of the store flew off the sill once again and crashed to the floor.

Everyone immediately looked toward the back of the store, but nobody was there.

"Oh, that's just our little goblin," one of the women said. "He's active tonight, isn't he?"

"Indeed," the other woman smiled.

U   U

Later that night, as I slept in an old hotel around the corner from the tack shop, I had a dream that Kathleen, who was staying in the room next to me, came knocking at my door to tell me she had a ghost in her room.

The next morning when Kathleen and I were setting up the P.A. for the clinic we were to do that day, she made an interesting statement.

"I've got this linen closet in my room," she said, just sort of out of the blue. "Last night I took a blanket out of it and closed the door tight. This morning when I got up, that door was open. Isn't that weird?"

Maybe …

U   U

A few years ago I was traveling from Tennessee to Maryland to work some horses. Being a Civil War buff, I stopped in Fredericksburg, Virginia, to have a look around. After coming out of the museum, I turned and started walking down a nearby street. I hadn't gone far when I noticed my lace-up boot had come untied.

Not thinking too much about it, I bent down, retied the lace, and continued my stroll down the street. I hadn't gone but twenty feet, when I looked down to find my boot lace untied again. Again, I reached down, tied it back up, and continued on my way. A little while later I reached a street corner and noticed once again that my boot had come untied.

Making a mental note not to buy that brand of boot lace ever again, I bent over one more time to retie my boot. As I was down on one knee tying the lace, a tour group crossed over to my side of the street. A number of the folks were smiling and one person, apparently the tour guide, asked if I was having trouble keeping my boots tied.

"A little," I answered, a bit perplexed by the question.

"So you see, folks," the guide said, turning to his charges, "our ghost works both sides of the street."

As the group passed, an older woman looked down at me with a grin.

"He was just telling us about the ghost that walks this street untying people's shoes," she said excitedly. "And lo and behold my husband's shoes came untied. Isn't that something?"

☙ ☙

Well, like I said, I don't believe in ghosts … never did. But I will say there are times here lately when a fella might just have to stop and wonder a little. And what the heck … wondering never hurt anybody.

CHAPTER 13

Sleigh Ride for the General

"It's only a big deal if you make it a big deal."

I was at the weekly Monday morning meeting for all the supervisors of the lodge, guest ranch, and conference center where I worked, and it looked as though we had a problem on our hands.

A large group of current and retired military personnel was checking in the next day for a conference that lasted until Sunday. That wasn't the problem. The problem was a winter storm that was supposed to hit the mountains, particularly our area, on Wednesday. That wouldn't have been much of an issue because, by then, all the folks attending the conference would already be here ... all the folks, that is, except one, the keynote speaker. A three-star general from Washington, D.C. was coming in Thursday morning, and the weather could certainly cause problems.

By Thursday, the storm was supposed to be in full swing, with very cold temperatures and snow accumulations measured in feet, not inches. If we got as much snow as the forecasters were predicting, the roads to our high-mountain lodge were going to be difficult to drive, at the very least. At worst, they might be impassable. Getting the general to the conference looked as though it was not going to be easy.

As we sat in the meeting, a number of ideas were discussed, but after an hour-and-a-half, nothing had been decided except that we'd wait another day, watch the weather forecast, and see just how bad the storm was supposed to get.

The next day brought good news and bad news. The bad news was that they were predicting even more snow than originally anticipated. The good news was that the army had found a way to get the general to the conference anyway. Perhaps it's more accurate to say that they had figured out a way to get him *close* to the conference. They would fly the general in on an army helicopter that would land in a big meadow about a mile or so away from the ranch. Now all we had to do was find a way to pick him up and get him to the lodge from there.

We held another meeting to discuss how we were going to do that. The obvious answer would be to drive our shuttle van down the highway to the neighbor's place, pick the general up, and bring him over to the conference. But if the roads were impassable, as they almost certainly would be, that option would go right out the window.

Someone suggested we pick him up with one of the lodge's snowmobiles, a viable option except the general was bringing with him an entourage of five to eight people. We only had three of our six snowmobiles working at the time, which meant we would have to make at least three trips (and maybe four or even five), in order to pick up everyone and their luggage and get them to the lodge. Some folks would have had to wait in the cold and snow while we shuttled others. With temperatures expected to be well below freezing, that pretty much eliminated that idea.

A few other options were suggested, including taking snowshoes over for the general and his staff and having them snowshoe back to the lodge. I'd kept pretty quiet until then, but when I heard that idea, I figured it was time to throw in my two-cents worth and propose the only thing that made sense to me.

"Why don't I just go over and pick them all up with the sleigh?" I suggested.

Quiet fell over the room as all heads turned in my direction. The looks on most faces told me the other supervisors didn't think much of my idea.

"The sleigh?" one of them said, almost in disgust. "You want to put a three-star general in a sleigh?"

"Why not?" I shrugged. "It holds twelve people—plenty of room for the general, his staff, *and* their luggage. We can take enough blankets with us that they could cover themselves from head to foot and stay warm."

The looks I was getting from the people around the table ranged from incredulous to mildly accepting.

"We'd easily be able to get them all from the helicopter in one trip, instead of several trips with the snowmobiles or having them freeze to death by making them walk over here in snowshoes."

The discussion went on a while longer, and in the end, the general manager decided our first option would be to pick up the general and his staff in the shuttle van. Our very distant second option would be to pick them up with the sleigh, but only if it was absolutely certain we couldn't get through with the van.

♘ ♘

As predicted, the temperature dropped considerably Wednesday morning, and by mid-afternoon heavy snow began to fall. Knowing I might need to get the sleigh ready first thing in the morning and knowing if I went home that night I might not be able to get back the next day, I decided to stay at the lodge overnight. I got up about 5:30 the next morning, and sure enough, we were right in the middle one of the biggest snowstorms in years.

There already was a good two-and-a-half feet of snow on the ground, with more on the way, and word had come from the highway department they were not going to plow the roads until later in the morning. We were going to have to use plan "B" for picking up the general, which meant I needed to get to work.

I went down to the shop, fired up one of the snowmobiles, and began packing the snow down to make a trail. I drove from the lodge, through the gate onto our neighbor's property, around a small group of trees, and finally into the big meadow where the helicopter would land in about four hours. I packed a trail wide enough to accommodate the big horses, as well as the runners of the sleigh, plus a little more. I drove the trail over and over for the next hour-and-a-half as the snow continued to fall. By the time I was finished, I had pretty effectively packed an area the size of a one-lane road from the ranch to the landing site.

I then cleaned off the sleigh, which was buried in snow, and started over to get the horses harnessed up. My assistant, Anne, had also stayed at the lodge overnight and was halfway finished harnessing the team by the time I got to the barn. We took the team to the sleigh, hooked them to it, placed our heavy (but portable) wooden steps on it, and drove the sleigh over to the landing site on a trial run.

The wooden steps were the ones we used for winter sleigh rides, and we took them over to make getting on the sleigh easier for the general and his staff. We'd go back and pick them up later.

More snow had accumulated on the trail I'd packed, so once we delivered the steps and got the team back to the lodge and in the barn, both Anne and I took snowmobiles out and repacked it. When we were finished with that, we re-hooked the team to the sleigh, cleaned it off one more time, and waited.

The general was to arrive at the landing site at exactly 9:00, and sure enough, about 8:55, we could hear the sound of the helicopter blades as the big chopper flew up the valley. We couldn't see the helicopter due to the lack of visibility, but we could tell as it flew over the lodge that it wasn't very high off the ground. Once the helicopter passed overhead, we waited until we heard the sound of the engine change in the distance, which told us it had gone from flying to landing, and we started over to the neighbor's place with the sleigh.

By the time the helicopter landed, the snow had subsided a little, and we made good time getting to the landing site. We pulled the rig around the grove of trees and into the meadow where the helicopter waited. At first the horses weren't sure what to think of the huge, green behemoth. Still, they responded nicely when I urged them forward, and we made a large loop in the meadow and stopped the sleigh near the helicopter, facing the direction of the lodge.

Anne jumped down, brushed the snow from the steps we'd dropped off earlier, and pushed them up next to the sleigh. One of the general's staff emerged from the helicopter.

"Excuse me," the captain said, as he approached. "Someone is supposed to be picking us up here."

"Yes, sir," I smiled. "That's us."

"I don't think you understand, son," the captain replied. "We've got a three-star general in there." He pointed his thumb over his shoulder at the helicopter. "He's expecting a warm vehicle to pick him up."

"Yes, sir," I said. "I know, but the roads are closed. We'll try to keep him comfortable and get you all over to the lodge as quick as we can."

"I'm going to need to speak to your boss," the captain said, obviously not happy with the situation.

"Captain!" A man in an army hat and overcoat climbed from the chopper. "What's the problem?"

"No problem, sir," the captain said, snapping around at attention. "We're just waiting for transport."

The man in the overcoat walked over to us. Then, looking the horses and the sleigh over carefully, a smile crossed his face.

"Why don't we just commandeer this outfit?" he asked, smiling up at me. "Would that be all right with you?"

"Yes, sir," I nodded. "That'd be just fine."

"Captain," he turned his attention back to the man standing by the sleigh, "let's go."

"Yes, sir," the captain snapped. He turned and ran back to the chopper. Four other men, all carrying bags of different shapes and sizes, climbed from the big green machine and headed toward us.

Within minutes, all the bags and men were loaded on the sleigh and covered with blankets. The man in the overcoat—the general—requested to sit in the front seat next to me, and I happily obliged him. Anne took a place in a seat just behind us.

I moved Diamond and Andy into a little trot as we pulled away from the chopper.

"We'll try to get you there as quick as we can, sir," I said, as we rounded the corner by the grove of trees and entered the small meadow.

"No hurry at all, son," the general said with a smile. "It's been years since I've had the opportunity to look at the backside of a good team. We used to farm with horses back when I was a kid, and this is quite a treat. I appreciate you doing this for us."

"No problem at all," I said, as I brought the team to a walk.

We took our time through the first part of the meadow, and the general asked me the horses' names, ages, and how long we'd had them. He was truly impressed with Diamond's size, as most folks are, and commented on how well behaved the team was while standing next to the helicopter.

"I'm not sure we could have ever gotten any of our teams that close to a Huey," he said. "You've definitely got a pair of real nice horses here."

"Yes, sir." Just then, an idea occurred to me. "They're pretty easy to get along with, if you'd care to take the lines for a bit."

"Really!" the general chirped, as if he were a kid who had just been told he was going to Disneyland. "I haven't had my hands on a set of lines in I don't know how long. Are you sure you wouldn't mind?"

"Not at all." And with that, I handed the general the lines.

At first he fumbled uncomfortably with them, as if trying to remember how to hold them properly. Then, as if someone flipped a switch, it all came back to him. He sat up straight, adjusted the lines between his fingers, moved the excess over to his left side, and settled in nicely.

The general drove the team through the meadow and around the corner toward the gate. When we were about 100 feet from the gate, he offered to hand the lines back to me.

"Go ahead," I smiled. "You're doing fine. This wouldn't be the first time you've taken a rig through a gate, would it?"

The general smiled. "No, it wouldn't."

With that, he stood up to get a better look at the gate and where the horses were in relationship to it. He slowed the team just a hair, gave them a little direction to the right to line them up better, and took us through the gate as though the last time he'd driven a team was yesterday.

I let him take the team and sleigh all the way to the front entrance of the lodge where he handed the lines back to me and, with a huge smile on his face, shook my hand.

"Thank you very much," he said. "That was a big thrill for me."

"Any time," I smiled.

The group, including the general, climbed down from the sleigh. The captain I spoke with earlier began brushing the snow from the general's coat. The general seemed more interested in petting Diamond on his head, which he did.

"Thanks again." The general smiled as he turned to head into the lodge.

"Hey, General," I called, just before he disappeared inside.

The general turned, almost causing the captain to run into him.

"If the army thing doesn't work out for you," I quipped, "come on back and I'll give you a job driving one of these teams."

"You know," the general laughed, "I just might take you up on that."

♘ ♘

The snow stopped later that day, and the weather turned warmer. On Saturday, the chopper returned to pick up the general and his crew, but by this time the roads were clear enough that the shuttle van was able to take them to it.

A few weeks later the lodge received an official letter from the general's staff thanking us for our hospitality, which the lodge framed and placed on the wall in the main lobby, along with an enlarged photo someone took that day of me standing on the sleigh, holding the lines, and talking to the general with the Huey helicopter behind us.

Two years later, out of the blue, I also received a letter. Mine, however, was from the general himself. In it he apologized for not writing sooner and then went on to thank me for allowing him to take the lines on that very snowy day in February two years earlier. He told me it had taken him back to his childhood and the days on the farm when he, his brothers, and his father spent long summer days driving and tending to the teams. In closing, he wished me well, thanked me again, and said he hoped our paths would cross again someday.

A lot of years have passed since that time, and while our paths haven't crossed, I still remember the look on the general's face when I handed him those lines. I think about how those men behind us on the sleigh that day must have seen him as a leader of uncompromising integrity and grit, one who commanded thousands and whose decisions shaped the outcomes of battles and even wars.

Yet, on that snowy day when I handed him the team, I saw something completely different. What I saw was an old teamster, someone who would always love having his hands on the lines and whose favorite job would always be sitting behind a good team of big horses.

CHAPTER 14

Sadie's Truck

*"It's never a good idea to touch a cowboy's hat,
pet his horse, or mess with his dog."*

Sadie was one of the friendliest dogs you'd ever want to meet. We got her as a tiny ball of black fur when she was about six weeks old. We were going to call her Shady or Shade for short, but our daughter Lindsey, who was about two years old at the time, couldn't yet pronounce the "sh" sound and so Shady quickly turned into Sadie.

Sadie was a cross between a black lab and a springer spaniel, and she came with me almost wherever I went. When we first got her, I was working as the livery supervisor at the guest ranch and lodge. Once Sadie learned her name and would come when she was called, I began taking her to work, and she soon became a favorite mascot of sorts with the employees.

While Sadie almost always stayed with me at the barn, she did begin to explore the property a bit as she got older, and not surprisingly, she discovered the back door to the kitchen. Eventually she figured out if she showed up at certain times of the day, she would catch the lodge's chef, Chef John, standing outside checking in a delivery, putting out the trash, or just taking a break.

Chef John epitomized what a chef should look like. He was very round (always the sign of a good chef), had a long handlebar moustache (the ends of which he waxed and curled to a point over his bulbous cheeks), and always wore a chef's hat, blouse, and apron (oftentimes even when he was off duty).

Sadie liked John. Not only because he was a pretty nice guy and always smelled like food, but also because he wasn't opposed to sneaking her a snack whenever she came around. Even though I asked Chef John not to feed her, he was so kindhearted he just couldn't help himself. As a result, it wasn't unusual to see the two of them sitting near the back door as he gave Sadie a small piece of prime rib, steak, chicken, fish, or pretty much anything else he happened to have around that day.

Along with cooking and eating, one of Chef John's true joys in life was betting on just about anything you could think of. And when I say he would bet on anything, I mean *anything*. Like a lot of folks, I suppose, he would bet on the outcome of sporting events with fellow employees or put a wager on the date of the birth of someone's baby. But Chef John also wasn't averse to betting a waitress whether or not one of her customers would be able to finish a particular meal, or how long it would take for someone to get back from the restroom, or how many glasses of wine someone would drink during dinner.

His bets sometimes bordered on the exotic. For instance, Chef John played a round of golf with my dad, my brother, and myself when my dad was in town for a visit (which was about the only time I *ever* played golf). My dad was one heck of a golfer (as was John), and not surprisingly, John convinced my dad to bet $5 on every hole. Unfortunately for John, my dad was on his game that day, and by the time we reached the 18th tee, my dad had won thirteen holes and John only four. John was into my dad for $45. On the last hole, John suggested they play for double or nothing—with the stipulation they play the entire hole, from tee to green, with their putters.

Well, much to John's chagrin, my dad parred the hole with four strokes, while John had seven. True to his word, John paid my dad the $90 he owed him on the spot and then took us all to the clubhouse and bought us lunch. That was just the kind of guy John was.

U U

Sadie and I were heading home from the lodge one evening, and as I drove past the American Legion Hall, I happened to notice Chef John's car in the parking lot. I decided to stop in for a quick beer and see what he was up to. I found John at the bar rolling dice with some of the other patrons and watching Monday Night Football. I pulled up a stool next to him, said hello to the folks I knew, ordered a beer, and decided to watch a little of the game before heading home for the night.

"Hey, Mark," John said, excusing himself from the dice game and turning to me. "You didn't happen to find my jacket in your truck, did you? I think I may have left it in there the other day."

I'd given John a ride to pick up his car from the garage, and he had indeed left his jacket in the back seat of my truck, a GMC one-ton pickup with a crew cab, the back seat of which Sadie used almost exclusively for her living quarters.

"Yeah, I did," I nodded. "It's out in the truck. I'll go get it for you."

"That's all right," he said, as he got up from his stool. "I'm on my way out anyway. I'll just grab it on my way to the car."

"Naw," I got up from the bar without having touched my beer. "I better get it for you. Sadie's in the truck, and she won't like you putting your hand in there."

"Sadie?" John smiled. "We're good buddies. She won't mind me getting my jacket."

"Actually, I think she will," I warned.

"No, she won't," John turned and started for the door.

"John," I said, with enough force to make him stop. "She doesn't like strangers messing with the truck when I'm not there. It'd be better if I go."

"Are you kidding me?" he smiled. "Sadie knows me. I feed her every day."

"That won't matter," I said matter-of-factly.

"I bet it will," he smirked.

"It won't."

"How much you want to bet?" he reached in his pocket and pulled out a money clip with a number of bills in it.

"How about we bet whatever hand you try to reach in there with?" I was half joking, half not.

"No, seriously," he said, thumbing through the bills. "How much? How about ten bucks?"

"How about fifty?" I said very quickly, hoping the confidence in my answer along with the bigger number would get him to drop the idea.

"Okay," he nodded. "Fifty. I'll be right back."

He turned and started for the door.

"Hold on, John, I was just kidding," I said, also starting for the door. "She won't let you in. I'll go get it."

"No," he said, holding up his hand for me to stop. "A bet is a bet."

"I was just kidding," I pleaded. "She won't let you in. I don't want you to get hurt."

"A bet's a bet," he repeated. And with that, out the door he went.

I shrugged my shoulders, went back to my stool, and sat down. The bartender, having overheard the entire conversation, came over.

"I got ten dollars says he gets the jacket out," he smiled.

"Okay," I shrugged.

A minute passed … then another and another. Before long, five minutes had gone by, then ten and fifteen. Still John had not come back in.

"You gonna go check on him?" the bartender asked.

"I'll give him a couple more minutes."

Another five minutes passed, and I decided it was time to make sure John still had all his body parts. I finished my beer, got up from my stool, and headed outside. What I found was the funniest thing I'd seen all day. There was John, laying face down on the roof of my truck, with all four of the truck doors wide open and Sadie sitting quietly in the back seat, right on top of John's jacket.

John slid cautiously to one side of the truck and slowly tried to ease his hand down into the back-seat compartment. With his fingers just barely visible to Sadie, she let loose with a barrage of vicious barking and snarling the likes of which even I'd never heard out of her before. John pulled his hand back with the speed of a rattlesnake's strike and then tried the same technique on the other side of the truck, resulting in the same response from Sadie.

Seeing as how Sadie appeared to have everything under control, I went back inside. Another twenty minutes would pass before John finally came back inside ... minus his jacket. He was peeling off five $10 bills from his money clip as he made his way over to me.

"I gotta get home," he said. There was a hint of defeat in his voice. "You wanna get my jacket for me?"

The whole bar burst out in laughter as he placed the fifty dollars in front of me.

"Hell, John," the bartender said, slapping another ten-dollar bill down in front of me. "I had ten bucks on you myself!"

"Well, I can tell you one thing," John fumed. "That's the last time I give *her* anything from *my* kitchen!"

John and I went out to the truck together. The doors were still wide open, and Sadie was sitting triumphantly on John's jacket. As we got to the truck, Sadie stood up and, wagging her tail, let John reach in and pull out his jacket. Sadie went over to him and began licking his face as if to say, *No hard feelings, John, I was just doing my job.*

U U

On the way home that night, Sadie and I did something we'd never done before. We went to one of those fast-food places, and each of us had a hamburger using the money she'd won for me in the one and only bet I ever had with Chef John.

And what about Sadie and John's relationship? Well, from what I understand, John tried very hard not to feed her when she came around to the back door of the kitchen. In the end, her big brown eyes won over John's soft heart, and it wasn't long before the two of them were once again sitting side by side behind the kitchen, with John slipping her treats.

One result of the episode was that word of John's inability to get his jacket out of my truck spread so quickly that I never again had to lock the doors of my truck, so long as Sadie was in it. Or maybe it would be more appropriate to say … I didn't have to lock the doors of *Sadie's* truck.

CHAPTER 15

Tyler's First Training Job

"You've got to control yourself before you can control your horse."

We usually began our morning at the guest ranch about 6:30. I started by getting on my horse, Buck, and riding out into the woods where our string of horses had been pastured for the night. Buck and I gathered the herd and brought them down to the catch pen near the barn. We let them in the barn to have their breakfast, brush and saddle them, and tie them to the hitch rails in preparation for the day's busy schedule of trail rides.

About 8:00 every morning, it was my son Tyler's job to go get the pony from his pen, lead him to the barn, and tie him up. He would very meticulously groom the little guy with a curry-comb and body brush and carefully saddle him for what was usually a full day of pony rides. Now this doesn't sound like a very hard job, and I suppose in the big scheme of things, it wasn't. But at seven years old, Tyler took the job very seriously. And why not? Until recently that very duty was being performed by one of our summer wranglers, Mandy, someone three times Tyler's age.

Tyler had always shown a strong interest in the goings-on at the barn, and early one morning he just showed up in his over-sized cowboy hat, boots, chinks, and jeans and started following Mandy around when she was getting the pony ready. As time went on, he began asking Mandy if he could lead the pony to the barn, and with Mandy's supervision, he did. Then he started grooming the pony with Mandy and eventually took on the saddling duties. It wasn't long before he just took over the job completely. For two or three weeks, Mandy stayed with him as he performed the task day in, day out, but it soon became clear he didn't need a whole lot of supervision. Before long he was doing the entire job by himself.

Tyler became pretty vigilant when it came to "his" pony, and he eventually took his duties one step further. Whenever someone came down to the barn for a pony ride, Tyler met him at the pony and made sure the youngster waited until a wrangler came to help. As the wrangler took the child for his ride, Tyler would walk alongside, often coaching the child on what he felt were the finer points of riding a good pony like the one he was in charge of.

On one morning when Tyler was leading the pony from his pen after the morning feeding, I had gone to start the tractor so I could harrow the riding arena. The tractor was parked about ten feet from the path Tyler was on, and it just so happened the two of them were walking past me when I fired up the old machine.

Normally, when I turned the key, the tractor turned over a few times and then quietly started up with very little complaining. But on this particular day, it let out one uncharacteristic and very loud backfire just as Tyler and the pony got next to it. Not surprisingly, the pony shied from the noise, and because Tyler didn't have a real firm grip on the lead rope (as he seldom needed to), the pony was able to pull away from him.

The pony didn't go far, just down to the barn where he stopped and waited for someone to come and get him. But it was clear Tyler was embarrassed by the fact the pony had gotten away from him. One of the wranglers caught the pony and gave him to Tyler, and I must say, what happened next truly surprised me.

I should explain that one of the things I did on the ranch was put on mini training clinics for the guests twice a week. These clinics were about an hour long, and I covered subjects like basic problem solving and sometimes things like colt starting.

I'd been doing these clinics for about two years, and in all that time I don't believe Tyler missed coming to more than two or three of them. Usually, he either sat on one of the benches and watched what was going on or sat in the dirt and played quietly by himself. As young a boy as he was at the time, I guess I never expected him to be paying much attention to what I was doing.

Well, it just so happened that the day the tractor backfired, we didn't have any pony rides scheduled (which never deterred Tyler from saddling the pony anyway). Instead of going through his usual saddling ritual, Tyler took the pony right down to the round pen and set to work training him to be ridden.

Of course the pony had already been ridden many times, insomuch as someone had been on his back while someone else led him around. But he had never been ridden without someone leading him. It was this fact Tyler had apparently set out to change.

The round pen was a good hundred yards from the barn area, out in a nice meadow. I'm sure Tyler thought he and the pony were all by themselves and nobody was watching them. That wasn't the case. Off and on over the next couple of hours, I peered through one of the barn windows and kept an eye on him, as he worked with the pony.

At first it was just fun to watch the two of them hanging out together. But as time went on, it was obvious Tyler was serious about the work he was doing. It was also very interesting for me to see him using a number of the same steps and ideas I used during the mini clinics—you know, the mini clinics I thought he wasn't paying attention to.

He started his session by teaching the pony how to turn and face him when he entered the pen. This was something he had seen me do countless times with horses we bought that were hard to catch. It amounted to teaching the horse that when someone stood either behind it or at its side, the horse should simply turn and face the person. It was a very low-stress way of helping the horse learn the basics of being caught, and apparently Tyler had been paying attention, because he had the pony turning toward him in less than fifteen minutes.

When he had successfully taught the pony to turn and face him, he went on to do a little longeing with him. When he was finished with that, he came up and got the pony's saddle and saddle pad, went back down to the pen, and saddled him the way he'd seen me saddling colts for the first time—very slowly and methodically.

He repeated each step several times and then came up and got the pony's little bridle, which we had never used. He returned to the round pen, and using the pony's lead rope, first gently slid the rope in and out of the pony's mouth to simulate the bit. After that, he gently slid the snaffle bit in and out of the pony's mouth several times. Finally, he put the bridle on the pony, again, just as he had seen me do on many occasions with a young horse.

Once saddled and bridled, Tyler led the pony around the pen for two or three laps. I would often do this with young horses before getting on them for the first time, and it must have been another thing he'd picked up on. Having done that, he took the pony to the middle of the pen, stopped him, and pulled on the pony's stirrup. This, too, was something I did with colts to help them set their feet and maintain their balance when a rider stepped in the stirrup for the first time.

Tyler then put his foot in the stirrup and lifted himself up several times without actually throwing a leg over. A few minutes later, he lifted himself up in the stirrup, laid his body over the saddle, and with his hand on the off side of the pony, moved the stirrup and tapped on the saddle leather, again all things I normally do with colts.

Finally, Tyler stepped up in the stirrup, threw a leg over, and sat quietly in the saddle for a few seconds before stepping off again. I usually did this with young horses to let them know that even though I was on their back, I wasn't going to live up there.

Evidently, Tyler had paid attention to that, too. After doing that three or four times, Tyler finally climbed on, settled in the saddle, and urged the little pony forward.

At first, I'm sure the pony had no idea what Tyler was asking from him. After all, he'd never been ridden without someone leading him. But Tyler continued to gently encourage the little guy, and before long the pony stepped off and started walking quietly around the pen. For the first few laps, Tyler didn't give the pony much guidance with the reins and just allowed him to wander around. Eventually, though, Tyler did pick up his reins and begin guiding the pony. Before long, he had the pony going forward, stopping, turning, and backing pretty well. It was then, I suppose, Tyler decided they both needed a break.

He got off, petted the pony generously on his head, took all the tack off him, and then led him back up to the barn.

"Whatcha doing, Ty?" I asked, as he and the pony came around the corner of the barn.

"Just working with this pony," he said, nonchalantly. "We're taking a break right now, though. We gotta get a drink."

He led the pony to the water tank and let him drink his fill. When he had finished, Tyler tied the pony in his usual spot and went to the little refrigerator we kept in the barn and opened up a can of Sprite. He tipped his hat back on his head and took a long drink from the can. He wiped his mouth with his sleeve and ended by letting out a little burp.

"So," I said, hoping to get some insight as to why he was doing all this work, "how's it going with him down there?"

"Goin' purty good." He took another long drink. "I should have him finished up by lunch, I think." He wiped his mouth with his sleeve.

Right then the phone rang. It was someone wanting to sign up for one of the morning rides, and as I took the reservation, Tyler finished his Sprite, let out another burp, and went back to work.

I ended up being pretty busy for the rest of the morning, so I wasn't able to keep track of the rest of his progress, although the wranglers did keep an eye on him for me when they could. About half an hour before lunch, Tyler brought the pony up from the round pen and into the arena. He mounted up and took the pony for a little ride, staying mostly in the walk, but also trotting from time to time.

The pony turned nicely when asked, stopped without too much trouble, and backed up pretty well. Just as Tyler finished up with his ride, the bell up by the dining room rang, telling us it was lunchtime.

Tyler pulled the pony's bridle and replaced it with the halter, loosened his cinch, and tied him up in his normal spot. The wranglers and I finished our morning chores and, along with Tyler, headed up for lunch.

We went through the lunch line, picked up our hamburgers and fries, and went into the dining room. Tyler and I sat next to each other, and because his burger was too big to get in his mouth, he asked if I'd cut it in half for him. Apparently starving to death, he picked up one half of the burger and eagerly went to eating.

"So," I said, as he chewed the food, "did you have a good morning with the pony?"

He nodded yes, but his mouth was so full he didn't dare try to speak.

"It looked like you did a pretty nice job with him," I commented, taking a bite of my own hamburger.

Tyler swallowed.

"Yup," he said. "He's doing good." He took another bite of his burger.

I was really impressed with the work Tyler had done with the pony that morning. He had been clear, concise, and thorough, and in the end, he had actually trained that little pony how to be ridden. But still, for the life of me, I simply could not figure out *why* he had done it.

Until then, Tyler's main interest in the pony had been his "job" of saddling him and getting him ready for the pony rides, not actually riding him. In fact, other than the first day I brought the pony home, Tyler had never asked to ride him. He'd been more interested in riding the bigger horses, so it was a wonderment to me not only that he spent so much time working with the pony, but also why he had been so meticulous in his work.

"You going to work the pony after lunch?" I asked.

"I don't know," he replied, sliding his last French fry through the puddle of ketchup on his plate and poking it in his mouth. "I think I want to go swimming with my new friends this afternoon."

"Well, I suppose that'd be okay," I nodded. "You worked pretty hard this morning."

"Yeah," he agreed. "But now he'll be better."

"Better?"

"Yeah," he said, taking a drink of milk and wiping his mouth with his sleeve. "Now he'll be like your horses."

"What do you mean?"

"Your horses don't run off when they hear loud noises," he said, sliding his chair away from the table and picking up his plate. "But you didn't train the pony. I don't want him running off like that, so I trained him like you do it. Now he won't do that no more."

He turned and started back toward the kitchen where he deposited his dirty plate.

"See you later, Dad," he said as he walked away. "I'm going swimming now."

U U

I've thought about that day a lot over the years and how easily Tyler turned a simple idea into reality. In his mind, he saw a certain quality to the horses on the ranch. One important part of that quality, as far as he was concerned, was that they didn't spook at loud noises. However, the one horse he was in charge of *did*, and that was just never going to do.

Rather than worrying about it or stressing over it or getting angry about it, he did something we adults often have trouble doing. He just fixed it the best way he knew how. Not only that, but after he had fixed it, he moved on to the next important thing in his day—going for a swim with his friends.

I often smile when I think about the very valuable lesson I learned from Tyler that day. It's a lesson that continues to stick with me.

Put simply: fix things that aren't right ... then go for a swim.

Mark Rashid, author of five best-selling books on horse training, has worked with horses since he was ten years old. His articles on solving problems from the horse's point of view have been published in *Western Horseman* and *Western Horse*. His successful horse clinics have been held across the United States and Europe. He lives near Estes Park, Colorado.